THE HERITAGE OF MODERN CRIMINOLOGY

Edited by

SAWYER F. SYLVESTER, JR.

SCHENKMAN PUBLISHING COMPANY
Cambridge, Massachusetts
Distributed by General Learning Press

Schenkman books are distributed by

General Learning Press
250 James Street
Morristown, New Jersey 07960

Copyright © 1972
Schenkman Publishing Company
Cambridge, Massachusetts

Library of Congress Catalogue Card Number: 72-81515
Printed in the United States of America

ALL RIGHTS RESERVED. THIS BOOK, OR PARTS THEREOF,
MAY NOT BE REPRODUCED IN ANY FORM WITHOUT
WRITTEN PERMISSION OF THE PUBLISHER.

TO

PROFESSOR ALBERT MORRIS

Acknowledgements

To Professors Charles Newman, Simon Dinitz, and Marshall Clinard, I wish to extend thanks for helpful advice and much-needed encouragement. I am indebted to Professor Leonard Savitz for providing me with a privately translated portion of the first edition of Lombroso's *L'Uomo Delinquente*. Finally, I should like to thank my resident editor and typist — and wife, Sheila.

Contents

Preface	xi
Introduction	1
Cesare Beccaria	9
On Crimes and Punishments	11
Adolphe Jacques Quetelet	25
Treatise on Man	27
Henry Mayhew	45
London Labor and the London Poor	47
Cesare Lombroso	63
Criminal Man	67
Gabriel Tarde	79
Penal Philosophy	81
Enrico Ferri	101
Criminal Sociology	103
Willem Adriaan Bonger	127
Criminality and Economic Conditions	129
Healy, Sellin & Sutherland:	
Early Twentieth Century American Criminology	149
The Individual Delinquent	
William Healy	151
Culture Conflict and Crime	
Thorsten Sellin	161
Principles of Criminology	
Edwin Sutherland	175
Bibliography	183

Preface

In teaching criminology to undergraduate students in a liberal arts college, I have often felt that the discipline had but an uneasy grip on the edge of the arts and sciences curriculum.

To the extent that criminology might limit itself to a mere cataloging of social problems with attendant solutions, this feeling would appear to be justified. The same might be said of sociology. However, as both of these fields presently involve consideration of theoretical systems as well as problems of general methodology, to that extent they have much of the same intellectual rigor of other sciences.

There is yet an additional phase in the development of both sociology and criminology which adds to their stature as academic subjects, and that is a study of their own intellectual history. Perhaps more of this has been done in sociology, but criminology has produced outstanding examples of historical scholarship, especially in the works of Leon Radzinowicz, Hermann Mannheim, and Harry Elmer Barnes.

In an attempt to supplement such historical discussions, I have provided here some examples of original writings by persons representing major periods in the early development of criminology. No attempt has been made to be comprehensive; that would have produced not a book, but an encyclopedia. My only intent has been to make more readily available to students in criminology part of their intellectual heritage.

S. F. S.

Introduction

William Maitland's phrase on the difficulties of writing history is perhaps overly quoted—but it is apt. "Such is the unity of all history that anyone who endeavors to tell a piece of it must feel that his first sentence tears a seamless web." Concern about the criminal offender and efforts to deal with him are found far back in history, long before there was any attempt to explain his behavior. Even efforts at explaining criminal behavior are found much earlier than many would see the beginnings of criminology as a science. These factors make establishing its precise origin difficult. Moreover, the various intellectual themes in criminology intersect at so many points throughout its development and have such active descendants at present, that use of any straight-line evolution model in cataloging its history is perilous.

Whatever these difficulties, however, there appears to be general agreement that criminology in the traditional sense began in the eighteenth century with the so-called "classical school." This school had two major sources: in part it resulted from the revulsion felt for the inhumanities of the *ancien régime* in Europe; in part it was the reigning philosophy of rationalism made manifest in jurisprudence. Criminal procedure in Europe at the time was a grim study in caprice and viciousness. Torture was commonly used to extract confessions, to force principals to implicate accessories, and to punish all parties either as a separate penalty or as an embellishment on the death penalty.

The practice of judicial limitation on the powers of the state to prosecute citizens was rare, and as a result the criminal law was widely used as a tool of political policy. Hence, the law was concerned not only with criminal behavior as such, but also with the extirpation of improper political and moral opinion. Without the protections of due process, persons were often accused on the word of *agents provocateurs*, charged secretly—often by use of the infamous *lettre de cachet*—kept in ignorance of the nature of the charges against them, tried in private, and finally subjected to punishments, the nature of which often seemed limited only by the ingenuity of the executioner.

In England, the judicial climate of the time was only slightly better. The scope of the death penalty had been extended to cover a vast number of criminal offenses, while its frequent application was often arbitrary and unequal. This situation was aggravated by the passage of a number of "emergency laws" requiring the death penalty, and also by the general lack of any secondary punishments.

It was an era of racing industrial revolution, enclosure movements, growing capitalism, and growing cities. Into these cities flowed the thousands torn from the common lands by the enclosure movements and drawn to the factories which employed all poorly, and many not at all. Large numbers of such people turned to crime as a way of life.

Not only was there no regular police force established to deal with such persistent, repetitive crime, but there was no body of knowledge concerning the causes of crime which might have suggested responses to it other than the death penalty. A popular answer to the problem of crime was the Doctrine of Maximum Severity, which stated that the purpose of punishment was not justice but prevention of crime, and therefore any means to that end was permissible. It was against these sorts of systems that the movement for penal reform was an anguished cry of protest.

The political writers of the Enlightenment distinguished man from the rest of the animal world by his ability to reason. Absolutely free in a state of nature, he had rationally given up, by means of a hypothetical agreement with his fellows, just so much of his previously unfettered freedom as would guarantee respect in the community for that which he retained. Beyond this, the law was to leave him alone. Moreover, that same rational ability allowed men to choose right over wrong. If they chose to do wrong, it was because they were able to see some advantage in it. The purpose of punishment, therefore, was to produce a situation wherein whatever natural benefit there might be in wrongdoing would be outweighed in the rational calculus.

Among those writers arguing for judicial change as part of a program of general social and intellectual liberalization were such outstanding figures as Voltaire and Montesquieu. In England, the voluminous works of Jeremy Bentham contained much on the subject of penal reform, including specific legislative proposals. He even designed a prison. It remained, however, for one of the lesser lights of the period to produce the most brilliant contribution to the literature of eighteenth century judicial liberalism: Cesare Beccaria. His book, *Dei Delitti et delle Pene* was the only major work of the time devoted solely to criminal justice; yet, it epitomized the spirit of the period, and its influence was far more widespread than its shy and retiring author ever anticipated.

Some may argue that the classical school was not properly a school of criminology but only of criminal jurisprudence since its emphasis was not on an empirical assessment of data, but on establishing the pre-eminence of certain social values. This position seems to have some support. The classical school did appear to make certain *a priori* assumptions concerning the nature of man, his free will, rationalism, and so forth. However, this may not totally condemn it to the realm of the unscientific because all sciences make some assumptions of necessity, which assumptions may forever remain unproved. Not to do so would create an infinite regress of colossal proportions.

At very least, we can say that classical criminology began a juridical tradition which continues unabated to this day. One may also suggest that, in a way, the classical school helped prepare the way for the more admittedly scientific schools which succeeded it. In pre-classical thought, the offender was one with the evil he represented. To rid the community of the evil, one usually had to get rid of the offender. It was not until the classical school split the vision of the criminal by insisting that he was, at one and the same time, (1) an offender against the community's mores, and (2) a citizen entitled to certain minimal rights, that the more empirical schools of criminology could see him as (1) an offender, and (2) an object of detached scientific study. It might also be suggested that the classical school took a liberal-humanist ethical position for which the more positivistic criminology of the next century was a system of justification or legitimation.

The beginnings of what would be admitted by all to be truly scientific criminology occurred in the early nineteenth century in France and Belgium. In an almost classic design for empirical research, two statisticians—Adolphe Jacques Quetelet and André Michel Guerry—sought for regularities in criminal behavior as they might appear in official statistics, specifically the *Compte Général de l'Administration de la Justice Criminelle en France*. With these data in mind, Quetelet and Guerry sought after statistics of other social factors occurring within the same geographical area from which the judicial statistics were obtained in an effort to demonstrate any concomitant variation which might exist.

The implications of these researches for criminology were far-reaching. For the first time, crimes were seen as social data, empirical facts capable of statistical representation and objective analysis. Moreover, both of these authors took the next step after correlational findings to explore the possibilities for social prediction. In addition, these early statistical studies can be viewed as an antecedent to the sociological studies of crime in the later nineteenth and early twentieth centuries. This can be seen especially in the relationship between the geographical concern of Guerry and Quetelet and the ecological emphasis of the Chicago school.

A considerable factual richness was added to the study of crime in the mid-nineteenth century by several authors who were apparently dissatisfied with mere enumerative description provided by the official statistical records of crime and of the conditions which led to it. H. A. Fregier in Paris and Henry Mayhew in London both wrote long and detailed descriptions not only of the incidence of criminal behavior, but of its quality, persistence, and patterning. Both knew their cities intimately and wrote with lavish detail on the conditions of poverty in the crowded lower classes and of responses to it by way of perpetual criminal ways of life. Such studies were the prelude to a view of criminal subcultures and persistent patterns of criminal behavior, not as social aberrations, but as constant and inevitable threads in the social fabric.

The most explicit expression of the claim that crime was a normal social phenomenon, however, was made by one whose prime interest was not criminology. One of Emile Durkheim's major goals seems to have been to establish sociology at the same level of positivistic rigor as he saw the rest of the sciences. To that end, it is said, he chose those subjects of study easily assumed to be the result of individual motivation—suicide and religion, for example—and proceeded to demonstrate unequivocally that they were the product of social forces. In the same manner, in an effort to establish the nature of social facts and the conditions of their normality, he chose crime as an example of something most people had assumed to be pathological and then proved with unassailable logic that it was normal. Not only did he show it to be normal, but suggested it was a functional part of any healthy social system.

Gabriel Tarde also represented the fast-growing discipline of sociology in nineteenth century France, but—unlike Durkheim—Tarde brought sociology to bear on criminal behavior as his principal interest. He also added an important degree of theoretical sophistication to the sociological study of crime. Up to this point, theories suggesting a sociological etiology tended to assume a direct relation between those social factors responsible for crime and the type of criminal behavior produced. For the most part they ignored the obvious fact that crimes are committed by individual human beings who, however much they may be influenced by their social milieu, do not respond to it as automatons. Social factors are filtered through individual consciousness and, by some process involving both the pre-existing individual and the new social experience, behavior is determined. Whatever one may think of Tarde's "laws of imitation," at least he provided one of the first suggestions for this intervening process.

At this time, however, the sociology of crime had acquired a persistent and attractive rival in the more clinical orientations of what came to be called the "positivist school." Interest became focused on the individual, not merely as an actor under the influence of criminogenic social facts, but as an organism predisposed to crime by some deep-seated anomaly of the soma or psyche. This interest in the biology and psychology of crime became so great that it seemed for a time almost to eclipse its sociological counterpart. To a degree, at least, it also put into the shade the development of an economic orientation toward crime, such as that represented by the writings of Willem Adriaan Bonger.

Of course, individualistic explanations of crime will generally be more ideologically popular since they tend to localize the source of a community's evil and to leave the legitimacy of the social and economic status quo unquestioned. Thus, the most threatening of criminological explanations, particularly in capitalist countries, might be the economic. This, coupled with the fact that Bonger, for example, was an avowed Marxist, would tend to make his theories something less than popular in early twentieth century America.

The biological and psychological setting for clinical criminology has its intellectual origins well back in the nineteenth century. The French psychiatrist, Esquirol, had published his *Traité des Maladies Mentales* in 1838; and the works of Gall and Spurzheim on phrenology had appeared even earlier. Rudolf Virchow propounded his theory of "organic regression" in his book *Cellular Pathology* in 1856; and Morel published *Treatise on Degeneracy* in 1857. But it was in 1859 that a work appeared which was to capture the scientific spirit of the times and to set the mold of much behavioral research for years to come—Darwin's *Origin of Species*.

In light of such a scientific trend, therefore, it ought not to appear unusual that when a physician and psychiatrist of this era sets out to find the causes of crime, he sought a clinical explanation based on an evolutionary model. In 1876, Cesare Lombroso published the first edition of *L'Uomo Delinquente*. This and subsequent works clearly made him one of the most controversial figures in the history of criminology. On the one hand, he has been referred to as "the father of modern criminology"; and, on the other hand, his primacy in this regard has been called a "myth."

Lombroso was the ultimate individualist in criminological theory, claiming at one point that the criminal was a separate sub-species of man, characterized by "atavism" and marked by a number of degenerative morphological features. However, in his later works, he became more and more eclectic, placing increased emphasis on social, economic, and other factors. His protégé, Enrico Ferri, placed even greater stress on such data, while remaining an ardent proponent of the positivist methodology which characterized Lombroso's work.

Whatever the limitations of some of the specific explanations of crime offered by what came to be called the "positivist school," it did serve to draw needed attention to the dynamics of the individual offender and to orient psychiatry and other clinical sciences to the problem of crime.

Moreover, the clinical orientation of the positivists was adopted by many who rejected their assumptions of biological degeneracy. Charles Goring, whose statistical studies in *The English Convict* were designed to refute Lombroso in his morphological findings, nevertheless adopted a distinctly individualist posture in regard to his own psychological theories. In America, Henry Goddard's studies of the influence of inherited feeble-mindedness on crime and William Healy's psychoanalytic approach to delinquency were similar examples of what came to be a widely accepted methodological approach.

It was also in America that the sociology of crime saw a renaissance. In the city of Chicago in the early twentieth century were found many of the social ills which had become characteristic of the large, rapidly expanding urban centers of the United States. And in the University of Chicago, there gathered a number of sociologists whose prime interest was the study of urban problems, such persons as William I. Thomas, Robert Ezra Park, Ernest Burgess, Nels Anderson, Louis Worth, and others. The writings of these were highly empirical within an ecological framework and heady in their descriptiveness.

Among those urban problems considered by the Chicago school were crime and juvenile delinquency; and two authors who made these areas their special concern were Frederick Thrasher and Clifford Shaw. Shaw notably made use of the concept of "delinquency areas," not in the remote statistical manner of the early nineteenth century criminal ecologists, but involving a "situational analysis," combining both a demographic view of social data as well as considerations of individual motivation.

More purely theoretical statements were made by such writers as Robert Merton, Thorsten Sellin, and Edwin Sutherland. The last of these formulated a series of propositions concerning the causes of criminal behavior which was to become one of the most famous statements in criminological theory. Sutherland's theory of "differential association" provides an explanation of the mechanism by which social factors are transmuted into individual criminal behavior by stating that such behavior is derived from a criminogenic milieu through the process of learning.

Sutherland himself states that he began his work in criminology at a time when the clinical approach in America as represented by Goddard and others and the sociological position of the Chicago writers were vying for primacy in the field. It seems incontestable that sociology has achieved that primacy, at least in American criminology. And yet, the tradition of judicial reform begun in the eighteenth century could not be more alive than in modern-day America; and developments in psychiatry and clinical psychology continue to offer tempting explanations of individual criminal dynamics. All in all, criminology has a rich heritage—and one made richer by its diversity.

CESARE BECCARIA
(1738–1794)

Cesare Bonesana, born in Milan of noble parentage on the fifteenth of March 1738, inherited the title Marchese di Beccaria—the name by which he has been known to history. He attended the Jesuit College at Parma where he was a notably undistinguished student. It has been suggested that his early restiveness under the dogmatic teachings of the good fathers contributed to the revolutionary quality of his later writings. However, the pattern of his later life, other than the production of his magnum opus, hardly encourages one to believe that he was broadly infected with the spirit of rebellion.

He became acquainted with Montesquieu's Lettres Persanes and the writings of the Encyclopedists on his return from college, and under the influence of their enquiring criticism entered upon the study of law at Pavia. In 1761, he married Teresa di Blasco, the daughter of a relatively impoverished military officer.

When not in devoted attendance on his new bride, Beccaria was much in the company of a band of Milanese youth known collectively as "The Academy of Fists." Talented, articulate, and thoroughly disenchanted with the literary and political condition of Italy, Beccaria and his companions—but mostly his companions—engaged in a number of efforts toward reform. Within this group, Beccaria was closest to the brothers Verri, Pietro and Alessandro. The former encouraged him in his study and writing in the field of judicial reform, and the latter was able to provide him with the raw data of the abuses present in the contemporary penal system by virtue of the fact that he held the position of Protector of Prisons.

In 1763, Beccaria began to work on Dei Delitti e delle Pene. He wrote occasionally and briefly on odd scraps of paper, constantly prodded along by Pietro Verri. The book was published in July of the next year and was an immediate success. Hailed by scholars and writers who were likewise at odds with the judicial abuses in Europe, the book can almost be seen as a focusing glass of eighteenth century dissident opinion. Beccaria was invited to France to commune with such luminaries as D'Alembert, Diderot, Helvetius, and D'Holbach. He visited them, but long before the visit was complete, he fled back to Milan to *his Teresa and a life of welcome obscurity. He never produced another work of any importance.*

Unlike Lombroso whose life was filled with scholarly enterprise a hundred years later, Beccaria seems much like a meteor whose brilliance, though intense, is soon burned out.

CESARE BECCARIA

On Crimes and Punishments

If we look into history we shall find that laws, which are, or ought to be, conventions between men in a state of freedom, have been, for the most part the work of the passions of a few, or the consequences of a fortuitous or temporary necessity; not dictated by a cool examiner of human nature, who knew how to collect in one point the actions of a multitude, and had this only end in view, *the greatest happiness of the greatest number*. Happy are those few nations who have not waited till the slow succession of human vicissitudes should, from the extremity of evil, produce a transition to good; but by prudent laws have facilitated the progress from one to the other! And how great are the obligations due from mankind to that philosopher, who, from the obscurity of his closet, had the courage to scatter among the multitude the seeds of useful truths, so long unfruitful!

The art of printing has diffused the knowledge of those philosophical truths, by which the relations between sovereigns and their subjects, and between nations are discovered. By this knowledge commerce is animated, and there has sprung up a spirit of emulation and industry, worthy of rational beings. These are the produce of this enlightened age; but the cruelty of punishments, and the irregularity of proceedings in criminal cases, so principal a part of the legislation, and so much neglected throughout Europe, has hardly ever been called in question. Errors, accumulated through many centuries, have never yet been exposed by ascending to general principles; nor has the force of acknowledged truths been ever opposed to the unbounded licentiousness of ill-directed power, which has continually produced so many authorised examples of the most unfeeling barbarity. Surely, the groans of the weak, sacrificed to the cruel ignorance and indolence of the powerful, the barbarous torments lavished, and multiplied with useless severity, for crimes either not proved, or in their nature impossible, the filth and horrors of a prison, increased by the most cruel tormentor of the miserable, uncertainty, ought to have roused the attention of those whose business is to direct the opinions of mankind.

The immortal Montesquieu has but slightly touched on this subject. Truth, which is eternally the same, has obliged me to follow the steps of that great man; but the studious part of mankind, for whom I write, will easily distinguish the superstructure from the foundation. I shall be happy if, with him, I can obtain the secret thanks of the obscure and peaceful disciples of reason and philosophy, and excite that tender emotion in which sensible minds sympathise with him who pleads for the cause of humanity.

OF THE ORIGIN OF PUNISHMENTS

Laws are the conditions under which men, naturally independent, united themselves in society. Weary of living in a continual state of war, and of enjoying a liberty, which became of little value, from the uncertainty of its duration, they sacrified one part of it, to enjoy the rest in peace and security. The sum of all these portions of the liberty of each individual constituted the sovereignty of a nation and was deposited in the hands of the sovereign, as the lawful administrator. But it was not sufficient only to establish this deposit; it was also necessary to defend it from the usurpation of each individual, who will always endeavour to take away from the mass, not only his own portion, but to encroach on that of others. Some motives therefore, that strike the senses were necessary to prevent the despotism of each individual from plunging society into its former chaos. Such motives are the punishments established against the infractors of the laws. I say that motives of this kind are necessary; because experience shows, that the multitude adopt no established principle of conduct; and because society is prevented from approaching to that dissolution, (to which, as well as all other parts of the physical and moral world, it naturally tends,) only by motives that are the immediate objects of sense, and which being continually presented to the mind, are sufficient to counterbalance the effects of the passions of the individual which oppose the general good. Neither the power of eloquence nor the sublimest truths are sufficient to restrain, for any length of time, those passions which are excited by the lively impressions of present objects.

CONSEQUENCES OF THE FOREGOING PRINCIPLES

The laws only can determine the punishment of crimes; and the authority of making penal laws can only reside with the legislator, who represents the whole society united by the social compact. No magistrate then, (as he is one of the society,) can, with justice, inflict on any other member of the same society punishment that is not ordained by the laws. But as a punishment, increased beyond the degree fixed by the law, is the just punishment with the addition of another, it follows that no magistrate, even under a pretence of zeal, or the public good, should increase the punishment already determined by the laws.

The sovereign, who represents the society itself, can only make general laws to bind the members; but it belongs not to him to judge whether any individual has violated the social compact, or incurred the punishment in consequence. For in this case there are two parties, one represented by the sovereign, who insists upon the violation of the contract, and the other is the person accused, who denies it. It is necessary then that there should be a third person to decide this contest; that is to say, a judge, or magistrate, from whose determination there should be no appeal; and this determination should consist of a simple affirmation or negation of fact.

OF THE INTERPRETATION OF LAWS

Judges, in criminal cases, have no right to interpret the penal laws, because they are not legislators. They have not received the laws from our ancestors as a domestic tradition, or as the will of a testator, which his heirs and executors are to obey; but they receive them from a society actually existing, or from the sovereign, its representative. Even the authority of the laws is not founded on any pretended obligation, or ancient convention; which must be null, as it cannot bind those who did not exist at the time of its institution; and unjust, as it would reduce men in the ages following, to a herd of brutes, without any power of judging or acting. The laws receive their force and authority from an oath of fidelity, either tacit or expressed, which living subjects have sworn to their sovereign, in order to restrain the intestine fermentation of the private interest of individuals. From hence springs their true and natural authority. Who then is their lawful interpreter? The sovereign, that is, the representative of society, and not the judge, whose office is only to examine if a man have or have not committed an action contrary to the laws.

In every criminal cause the judge should reason syllogistically. The *major* should be the general law; the *minor*, the conformity of the action, or its opposition to the laws; the *conclusion*, liberty, or punishment. If the judge be obliged by the imperfection of the laws, or chooses to make any other or more syllogisms than this, it will be an introduction to uncertainty.

There is nothing more dangerous than the common axiom, *the spirit of the laws is to be considered.* To adopt it is to give way to the torrent of opinions. This may seem a paradox to vulgar minds, which are more strongly affected by the smallest disorder before their eyes, than by the most pernicious though remote consequences produced by one false principle adopted by a nation.

The disorders that may arise from a rigorous observance of the letter of penal laws are not to be compared with those produced by the interpretation of them. The first are temporary inconveniences which will oblige the legislature to correct the letter of the law, the want of preciseness and uncertainty of which has occasioned these disorders; and this will put a stop to the fatal liberty of explaining, the source of arbitrary and venal declamations. When the code of laws is once fixed, it should be observed in the literal sense, and nothing more is left to the judge than to determine whether an action be or be not conformable to the written law. When the rule of right, which ought to direct the actions of the philosopher, as well as the ignorant, is a matter of controversy, not of fact, the people are slaves to the magistrates. The despotism of this multitude of tyrants is more insupportable the less the distance is between the oppressor and the oppressed, more fatal than that of one, for the tyranny of many is not to be shaken off but by having recourse to that of one alone. It is more cruel, as it meets with more opposition, and the cruelty of a tyrant is not in proportion to his strength, but to the obstacles that oppose him.

OF THE OBSCURITY OF LAWS

If the power of interpreting laws be an evil, obscurity in them must be another, as the former is the consequence of the latter. This evil will be still greater if the laws be written in a language unknown to the people; who, being ignorant of the consequences of their own actions, become necessarily dependent on a few, who are interpreters of the laws, which, instead of being public and general, are thus rendered private and particular. What must we think of mankind when we reflect, that such is the established custom of the greatest part of our polished and enlightened Europe? Crimes will be less frequent in proportion as the code of laws is more universally read and understood; for there is no doubt but that the eloquence of the passions is greatly assisted by the ignorance and uncertainty of punishments.

Hence it follows, that, without written laws, no society will ever acquire a fixed form of government, in which the power is vested in the whole, and not in any part of the society; and in which the laws are not to be altered but by the will of the whole, nor corrupted by the force of private interest. Experience and reason show us that the probability of human traditions diminishes in proportion as they are distant from their sources. How then can laws resist the inevitable force of time, if there be not a lasting monument of the social compact.

OF THE PROPORTION BETWEEN CRIMES AND PUNISHMENTS

It is not only the common interest of mankind that crimes should not be committed, but that crimes of every kind should be less frequent, in proportion to the evil they produce to society. Therefore the means made use of by the legislature to prevent crimes should be more powerful, in proportion as they are destructive of the public safety and happiness, and as the inducements to commit them are stronger. Therefore there ought to be a fixed proportion between crimes and punishments.

It is impossible to prevent entirely all the disorders which the passions of mankind cause in society. These disorders increase in proportion to the number of people and the opposition of private interests. If we consult history, we shall find them increasing, in every state, with the extent of dominion. In political arithmetic, it is necessary to substitute a calculation of probabilities to mathematical exactness. That force which continually impels us to our own private interest, like gravity, acts incessantly, unless it meets with an obstacle to oppose it. The effects of this force are the confused series of human actions. Punishments, which I would call political obstacles, prevent the fatal effects of private interest, without destroying the impelling cause, which is that sensibility inseparable from man. The legislator acts, in this case, like a skilful architect, who endeavours to counteract the force of gravity by combining the circumstances which may contribute to the strength of his edifice.

The necessity of uniting in society being granted, together with the conventions which the opposite interests of individuals must necessarily require, a scale of crimes may be formed, of which the first degree should consist of those which immediately tend to the dissolution of society, and the last of the smallest possible injustice done to a private member of that society. Between these extremes will be comprehended all actions contrary to the public good which are called criminal, and which descend by insensible degrees, decreasing from the highest to the lowest. If mathematical calculation could be applied to the obscure and infinite combinations of human actions, there might be a corresponding scale of punishments, descending from the greatest to the least; but it will be sufficient that the wise legislator mark the principal divisions, without disturbing the order, lest to crimes of the *first* degree be assigned punishments of the *last*. If there were an exact and universal scale of crimes and punishments, we should there have a common measure of the degree of liberty and slavery, humanity and cruelty of different nations.

OF EVIDENCE AND THE PROOFS OF A CRIME, AND OF THE FORM OF JUDGMENT

That certainty which is necessary to decide that the accused is guilty is the very same which determines every man in the most important transactions of his life.

But it is much easier to feel this moral certainty of proofs than to define it exactly. For this reason, I think it an excellent law which establishes assistants to the principal judge, and those chosen by lot; for that ignorance which judges by its feelings is less subject to error than the knowledge or the laws which judges by opinion. Where the laws are clear and precise, the office of the judge is merely to ascertain the fact. If, in examining the proofs of a crime, acuteness and dexterity be required, if clearness and precision be necessary in summoning up the result, to judge of the result itself nothing is wanting but plain and ordinary good sense, a less fallacious guide than the knowledge, of a judge, accustomed to find guilty, and to reduce all things to an artificial system borrowed from his studies. Happy the nation where the knowledge of the law is not a science!

It is an admirable law which ordains that every man shall be tried by his peers; for, when life, liberty and fortune, are in question, the sentiments which a difference of rank and fortune inspires should be silent; that superiority with which the fortunate look upon the unfortunate, and that envy with which the inferior regard their superiors, should have no influence. But when the crime is an offence against a fellow-subject, one half of the judges should be peers to the accused, and the other peers to the person offended: so that all private interest, which, in spite of ourselves, modifies the appearance of objects, even in the eyes of the most equitable, is counteracted, and nothing remains to turn aside the direction of truth and the laws. It is also just that the accused should have the liberty of excluding a certain number of his judges; where this liberty is enjoyed for a long time, without any instance to the contrary, the criminal seems to condemn himself.

All trials should be public, that opinion, which is the best, or perhaps the only cement of society, may curb the authority of the powerful, and the passions of the judge, and that the people may say, 'We are protected by the laws; we are not slaves:' a sentiment which inspires courage, and which is the best tribute to a sovereign who knows his real interest.

OF SECRET ACCUSATIONS

Secret accusations are a manifest abuse, but consecrated by custom in many nations, where, from the weakness of the government, they are necessary. This custom makes men false and treacherous. Whoever suspects another to be an informer, beholds in him an enemy; and from thence mankind are accustomed to disguise their real sentiments; and, from the habit of concealing them from others, they at last even hide them from themselves. Unhappy are those who have arrived at this point! without any certain and fixed principles to guide them, they fluctuate in the vast sea of opinion, and are busied only in escaping the monsters which surround them: to those the present is always embittered by the uncertainty of the future; deprived of the pleasures of tranquillity and security, some fleeting moments of happiness, scattered thinly through their wretched lives, console them for the misery of existing. Shall we, amongst such men, find intrepid soldiers, to defend their king and country? Amongst such men shall we find incorruptible magistrates, who, with the spirit of freedom and patriotic eloquence, will support and explain the true interest of their sovereign; who, with the tributes, offer up at the throne the love and blessing of the people, and thus bestow on the palaces of the great and the humble cottage peace and security, and to the industrious a prospect of bettering their lot that useful ferment and vital principle of states?

Who can defend himself from calumny, armed with that impenetrable shield of tyranny, secrecy? What a miserable government must that be where the sovereign suspects an enemy in every subject, and, to secure the tranquillity of the public, is obliged to sacrifice the repose of every individual.

OF TORTURE

The torture of a criminal during the course of his trial is a cruelty consecrated by custom in most nations. It is used with an intent either to make him confess his crime, or to explain some contradictions into which he had been led during his examination, or discover his accomplices, or for some kind of metaphysical and incomprehensible purgation of infamy, or, finally, in order to discover other crimes of which he is not accused, but of which he may be guilty.

No man can be judged a criminal until he be found guilty; nor can society take from him the public protection until it have been proved that he has violated the conditions on which it was granted. What right, then, but that of power, can authorise the punishment of a citizen so long as there remains any doubt of his guilt? This dilemma is frequent.

Either he is guilty, or not guilty. If guilty, he should only suffer the punishment ordained by the laws, and torture becomes useless, as his confession is unnecessary. If he be not guilty, you torture the innocent; for, in the eye of the law, every man is innocent whose crime has not been proved. Besides, it is confounding all relations to expect that a man should be both the accuser and accused; and that pain should be the test of truth, as if truth resided in the muscles and fibres of a wretch in torture. By this method the robust will escape, and the feeble be condemned. These are the inconveniencies of this pretended test of truth, worthy only of a cannibal, and which the Romans, in many respects barbarous, and whose savage virtue has been too much admired, reserved for the slaves alone.

Every act of the will is invariably in proportion to the force of the impression on our senses. The impression of pain, then, may increase to such a degree, that, occupying the mind entirely, it will compel the sufferer to use the shortest method of freeing himself from torment. His answer, therefore, will be an effect as necessary as that of fire or boiling water, and he will accuse himself of crimes of which he is innocent: so that the very means employed to distinguish the innocent from the guilty will most effectually destroy all difference between them.

A very strange but necessary consequence of the use of torture is, that the case of the innocent is worse than that of the guilty. With regard to the first, either he confesses the crime which he has not committed, and is condemned, or he is acquitted, and has suffered a punishment he did not deserve. On the contrary, the person who is really guilty has the most favourable side of the question; for, if he supports the torture with firmness and resolution, he is acquitted, and has gained, having exchanged a greater punishment for a less.

OF THE ADVANTAGE OF IMMEDIATE PUNISHMENT

The more immediately after the commission of a crime a punishment is inflicted, the more just and useful it will be. It will be more just, because it spares the criminal the cruel and superfluous torment of uncertainty, which increases in proportion to the strength of his imagination and the sense of his weakness; and because the privation of liberty, being a punishment, ought to be inflicted before condemnation but for as short a time as possible. Imprisonment, I say, being only the means of securing the person of the accused until he be tried, condemned, or acquitted, ought not only to be of as short duration, but attended with as little severity as possible. The time should be determined by the necessary preparation for the trial, and the right of priority in the oldest prisoners. The confinement ought not to be closer than is requisite to prevent his flight, or his concealing the proofs of the crime; and the trial should be conducted with all possible expedition. Can there be a more cruel contrast than that between the indolence of a judge and the painful anxiety of the accused; the comforts and pleasures of an insensible magistrate, and the filth and misery of the prisoner? In general, as I have before observed, *The degree of the punishment, and the consequences of a crime, ought to be so contrived as to have the greatest possible effect on others, with the least possible pain to the delinquent.* If there be any society in which this is not a fundamental principle, it is an unlawful society; for mankind, by their union, originally intended to subject themselves to the least evils possible.

An immediate punishment is more useful; because the smaller the interval of time between the punishment and the crime, the stronger and more lasting will be the association of the two ideas of *crime* and *punishment*; so that they may be considered, one as the cause, and the other as the unavoidable and necessary effect. It is demonstrated, that the association of ideas is the cement which unites the fabric of the human intellect, without which pleasure and pain would be simple and ineffectual sensations.

It is, then, of the greatest importance that the punishment should succeed the crime as immediately as possible, if we intend that, in the rude minds of the multitude, the seducing picture of the advantage arising from the crime should instantly awake the attendant idea of punishment. Delaying the punishment serves only to separate these two ideas, and thus affects the minds of the spectators rather as being a terrible sight than the necessary consequence of a crime, the horror of which should contribute to heighten the idea of the punishment.

OF THE MILDNESS OF PUNISHMENTS

Crimes are more effectually prevented by the *certainty* than the *severity* of punishment. Hence in a magistrate the necessity of vigilance, and in a judge of implacability, which, that it may become an useful virtue, should be joined to a mild legislation. The certainty of a small punishment will make a stronger impression than the fear of one more severe, if attended with the hopes of escaping; for it is the nature of mankind to be terrified at the approach of the smallest inevitable evil, whilst hope, the best gift of Heaven, hath the power of dispelling the apprehension of a greater, especially if supported by examples of impunity, which weakness or avarice too frequently afford.

If punishments be very severe, men are naturally led to the perpetration of other crimes, to avoid the punishment due to the first. The countries and times most notorious for severity of punishments were always those in which the most bloody and inhuman actions and the most atrocious crimes were committed; for the hand of the legislator and the assassin were directed by the same spirit of ferocity, which on the throne dictated laws of iron to slaves and savages, and in private instigated the subject to sacrifice one tyrant to make room for another.

In proportion as punishments become more cruel, the minds of men, as a fluid rises to the same height with that which surrounds it, grow hardened and insensible; and the force of the passions still continuing, in the space of an hundred years the *wheel* terrifies no more than formerly the *prison*. That a punishment may produce the effect required, it is sufficient that the *evil* it occasions should exceed the *good* expected from the crime, including in the calculation the certainty of the punishment, and the privation of the expected advantage. All severity beyond this is superfluous, and therefore tyrannical.

OF THE PUNISHMENT OF DEATH

The useless profusion of punishments, which has never made men better, induces me to inquire, whether the punishment of *death* be really just or useful in a well governed state? What *right*, I ask, have men to cut the throats of their fellow-creatures? Certainly not that on which the sovereignty and laws are founded. The laws, as I have said before, are only the sum of the smallest portions of the private liberty of each individual, and represent the general will, which is the aggregate of that of each individual. Did any one ever give to others the right of taking away his life? Is it possible that, in the smallest portions of the liberty of each, sacrificed to the good of the public, can be contained the greatest of all good, life? If it were so, how shall it be reconciled to the maxim which tells us, that a man has no right to kill himself, which he certainly must have, if he could give it away to another?

But the punishment of death is not authorised by any right; for I have demonstrated that no such right exists. It is therefore a war of a whole nation against a citizen, whose destruction they consider as necessary or useful to the general good. But if I can further demonstrate that it is neither necessary nor useful, I shall have gained the cause of humanity.

The death of a citizen cannot be necessary but in one case: when, though deprived of his liberty, he has such power and connections as may endanger the security of the nation; when his existence may produce a dangerous revolution in the established form of government.

But, even in this case, it can only be necessary when a nation is on the verge of recovering or losing its liberty, or in times of absolute anarchy, when the disorders themselves hold the place of laws: but in a reign of tranquillity, in a form of government approved by the united wishes of the nation, in a state well fortified from enemies without and supported by strength within, and opinion, perhaps more efficacious, where all power is lodged in the hands of a true sovereign, where riches can purchase pleasures and not authority, there can be no necessity for taking away the life of a subject.

If the experience of all ages be not sufficient to prove, that the punishment of death has never prevented determined men from injuring society, if the example of the Romans, if twenty years' reign of Elizabeth, empress of Russia, in which she gave the fathers of their country an example more illustrious than many conquests bought with blood; if, I say, all this be not sufficient to persuade mankind, who always suspect the voice of reason, and who choose rather to be led by authority, let us consult human nature in proof of my assertion.

It is not the intenseness of the pain that has the greatest effect on the mind, but its continuance; for our sensibility is more easily and more powerfully affected by weak but repeated impressions, than by a violent but momentary impulse. The power of habit is universal over every sensible being. As it is by that we learn to speak, to walk, and to satisfy our necessities, so the ideas of morality are stamped on our minds by repeated impressions. The death of a criminal is a terrible but momentary spectacle, and therefore a less efficacious method of deterring others than the continued example of a man deprived of his liberty, condemned, as a beast of burden, to repair, by his labour, the injury he has done to society, *If I commit such a crime,* says the spectator to himself, *I shall be reduced to that miserable condition for the rest of my life.* A much more powerful preventive than the fear of death which men always behold in distant obscurity.

Let us, for a moment, attend to the reasoning of a robber or assassin, who is deterred from violating the laws by the gibbet or the wheel. I am sensible, that to develop the sentiments of one's own heart is an art which education only can teach; but although a villain may not be able to give a clear account of his principles, they nevertheless influence his conduct. He reasons thus: 'What are these laws that I am bound to respect, which make so great a difference between me and the rich man? He refuses me the farthing I ask of him, and excuses himself by bidding me have recourse to labour, with which he is unacquainted.

'Who made these laws? The rich and the great, who never deigned to visit the miserable hut of the poor, who have never seen him dividing a piece of mouldy bread, amidst the cries of his famished children and the tears of his wife. Let us break those ties, fatal to the greatest part of mankind, and only useful to a few indolent tyrants. Let us attack injustice at its source. I will return to my natural state of independence. I shall live free and happy on the fruits of my courage and industry. A day of pain and repentance may come, but it will be short; and for an hour of grief I shall enjoy years of pleasure and liberty. King of a small number as determined as myself, I will correct the mistakes of fortune, and I shall see those tyrants grow pale and tremble at the sight of him, whom, with insulting pride, they would not suffer to rank with their dogs and horses.'

The punishment of death is pernicious to society, from the example of barbarity it affords. If the passions, or the necessity of war, have taught men to shed the blood of their fellow creatures, the laws, which are intended to moderate the ferocity of mankind, should not increase it by examples of barbarity, the more horrible as this punishment is usually attended with formal pageantry. Is it not absurd, that the laws, which detest and punish homicide, should, in order to prevent murder, publicly commit murder themselves? What are the true and most useful laws? Those compacts and conditions which all would propose and observe in those moments when private interest is silent, or combined with that of the public. What are the natural sentiments of every person concerning the punishment of death? We may read them in the contempt and indignation with which every one looks on the executioner, who is nevertheless an innocent executor of the public will, a good citizen, who contributes to the advantage of society, the instrument of the general security within, as good soldiers are without. What then is the origin of this contradiction? Why is this sentiment of mankind indelible to the scandal of reason? It is, that, in a secret corner of the mind, in which the original impressions of nature are still preserved, men discover a sentiment which tells them, that their lives are not lawfully in the power of any one, but of that necessity only which with its iron sceptre rules the universe.

OF THE MEANS OF PREVENTING CRIMES

It is better to prevent crimes than to punish them. This is the fundamental principle of good legislation, which is the art of conducting men to the *maximum* of happiness, and to the *minimum* of misery, if we may apply this mathematical expression to the good and evil of life. But the means hitherto employed for that purpose are generally inadequate, or contrary to the end proposed. It is impossible to reduce the tumultuous activity of mankind to absolute regularity; for, amidst the various and opposite attractions of pleasure and pain, human laws are not sufficient entirely to prevent disorders in society. Such, however is the chimera of weak men, when invested with authority. To prohibit a number of indifferent actions is not to prevent the crimes which they may produce, but to create new ones, it is to change at will the ideas of virtue and vice, which, at other times, we are told, are eternal and immutable. To what a situation should we be reduced if every thing were to be forbidden that might possibly lead to a crime? We must be deprived of the use of our senses: for one motive that induces a man to commit a real crime, there are a thousand which excite him to those indifferent actions which are called crimes by bad laws. If then the probability that a crime will be committed be in proportion to the number of motives, to extend the sphere of crimes will be to increase that probability. The generality of laws are only exclusive privileges, the tribute of all to the advantages of a few.

Would you prevent crimes? Let the laws be clear and simple, let the entire force of the nation be united in their defence, let them be intended rather to favour every individual than any particular classes of men, let the laws be feared, and the laws only. The fear of the laws is salutary, but the fear of men is a fruitful and fatal source of crimes. Men enslaved are more voluptuous, more debauched, and more cruel than those who are in a state of freedom. These study the sciences, the interest of nations, have great objects before their eyes, and imitate them; but those, whose views are confined to the present moment, endeavour, amidst the distraction of riot and debauchery, to forget their situation; accustomed to the uncertainty of all events, for the laws determine none, the consequences of their crimes become problematical, which gives an additional force to the strength of their passions.

OF THE SCIENCES

Would you prevent crimes? Let liberty be attended with knowledge. As knowledge extends, the disadvantages which attend it diminish and the advantages increase. A daring impostor, who is always a man of some genius, is adored by the ignorant populace, and despaired by men of understanding. Knowledge facilitates the comparison of objects, by shewing them in different points of view. When the clouds of ignorance are dispelled by the radiance of knowledge, authority trembles, but the force of the laws remains immoveable. Men of enlightened understanding must necessarily approve those useful conventions which are the foundation of public safety; they compare with the highest satisfaction, the inconsiderable portion of liberty of which they are deprived with the sum total sacrificed by others for their security; observing that they have only given up the pernicious liberty of injuring their fellow-creatures, they bless the throne, and the laws upon which it is established.

CONCLUSION

From what I have written results the following general theorem, of considerable utility, though not conformable to custom, the common legislator of nations:

That a punishment may not be an act of violence, of one, or of many, against a private member of society, it should be public, immediate, and necessary, the least possible in the case given, proportioned to the crime, and determined by the laws.

ADOLPHE JACQUES QUETELET
(1796–1874)

Adolphe Quetelet was born in the town of Ghent on the twenty-second of February, 1796. He was educated in the Lyceum there and after his graduation spent a year teaching mathematics in a private school in Audenaerde. At nineteen, he was made Instructor at a newly formed college in Ghent from which he was the first to receive the degree of Doctor of Science in 1819. In this same year he accepted the chair in elementary mathematics at the Athenaeum in Brussels, and four years thereafter was made Professor in higher mathematics at the same institution.

During his tenure at the Athenaeum, among other accomplishments, Quetelet was principally responsible for the revitalization of the Royal Academy of Science and Literature which had fallen on hard times. It was during this period as well that, while visiting Paris to seek advice on the subject of astronomical instruments for a proposed observatory, he came under the influence of the mathematician Laplace, whose emphasis on the theory of probabilities is thought to have been among the most important early influences on Quetelet's subsequent works. Increasingly, thereafter, Quetelet insisted that scientific laws—even in such seemingly exact fields as astronomy—could be observed to hold only within certain degrees of probability, and that such laws applied to and reflected large numbers of observations and not individual occurrences.

Because of this belief, Quetelet recommended that any description of astronomical data be the result of a large number of observations of the same occurrence from different sites. Likewise, any statement as to the correlation of meteorological, astronomical, and other data may be established only after repeated observations and then only within certain limits of error.

It was precisely in this philosophical and scientific frame of mind that Quetelet approached the study of social data. What he called "moral statistics" referred to those areas in volitional human behavior wherein there were perceived regularities (such as marriage, suicide, and crime); and the instruments for making such regularities perceptible were the same statistical devices which had produced similar patterns in his astronomical and meteorological observations. Having once established mathematical norms of social behavior, Quetelet felt that one may then correlate these data or relate them to other nonsocial data.

Although August Comte's *"positivism"* is often cited as the beginning of a science of society, the statistics of Quetelet are probably closer to modern sociology than the rambling philosophy of his more famous colleague. Certain it is that his studies of moral statistics stand at the beginning of a scientific study of crime.

Quetelet dealt with the subject of crime in several of his writings, but the third chapter of his Treatise on Man *is concerned exclusively with the subject.*

ADOLPHE JACQUES QUETELET

Treatise on Man

OF CRIMES IN GENERAL AND OF THE REPRESSION OF THEM

Supposing men to be placed in similar circumstances, I call the greater or less probability of committing crime, the *propensity to crime*. My object is more especially to investigate the influence of season, climate, sex, and age, on this propensity.

I have said that the circumstances in which men are placed ought to be similar, that is to say, equally favourable, both in the existence of objects likely to excite the propensity and in the facility of committing the crime. It is not enough that a man may merely have the intention to do evil, he must also have the opportunity and the means. Thus the propensity to crime may be the same in France as in England, without, on that account, the *morality* of the nations being the same. I think this distinction of importance.

[T]his is also the place to examine a difficulty which has not escaped M. Alphonse de Candolle: it is this, that our observations can only refer to *a certain number of known and tried offences, out of the unknown sum total of crimes committed.* Since this sum total of crimes committed will probably ever continue unknown, all the reasoning of which it is the basis will be more or less defective. I do not hesitate to say, that all the knowledge which we possess on the statistics of crimes and offences will be of no utility whatever, unless we admit without question that *there is a ratio, nearly invariably the same, between known and tried offences and the unknown sum total of crimes committed.* This ratio is necessary, and if it did not really exist, every thing which, until the present time, has been said on the statistical documents of crime, would be false and absurd. We are aware, then, how important it is to legitimate such a ratio, and we may be astonished that this has not been done before now. The ratio of which we speak necessarily varies according to the nature and seriousness of the crimes: in a well-organised society, where the police is active and justice is rightly administered, this ratio, for murders and assassinations, will be nearly equal to unity; that is to say, no individual will disappear from the society by murder or assassination, without its being known; this will not be precisely the case with poisonings. When we look to thefts and offences of smaller importance, the ratio will become very small, and a great number of offences will remain unknown, either because those against whom they are committed do not perceive them, or do not wish to prosecute the perpetrators, or because justice itself has not sufficient evidence to act upon. Thus, the greatness of this ratio, which will generally be different for different crimes and offences, will chiefly depend on the activity of justice in reaching the guilty, on the care with which the latter conceal themselves, on the repugnance which the individuals injured may have to complain, or perhaps on their not knowing that any injury has been committed against them. Now, if all the causes which influence the magnitude of the ratio remain the same, we may also assert that the effects will remain invariable. This result is confirmed in a curious manner by induction, and observing the surprising constancy with which the numbers of the statistics of crime are reproduced annually— a constancy which, no doubt, will be also reproduced in the numbers at which we cannot arrive: thus, although we do not know the criminals who escape justice, we very well know that every year between 7000 and 7300 persons are brought before the criminal courts, and that 61 are regularly condemned out of every 100; that 170,000 nearly are brought before courts of correction, and that 85 out of 100 are condemned; and that, if we pass to details, we find a no less alarming regularity; thus we find that between 100 and 150 individuals are annually condemned to death, 280 condemned to perpetual hard labour, 1050 to hard labour for a time, 1220 to solitary confinement (*à la réclusion*), &c.; so that this budget of the scaffold and the prisons is discharged by the French nation, with much greater regularity, no doubt, than the financial budget; and we might say, that what annually escapes the minister of justice is a more regular sum than the deficiency of revenue to the treasury.

I shall commence by considering, in a general manner, the propensity to crime in France, availing myself of the excellent documents contained in the *Comptes Généraux de l'Administration de la Justice of* this country; I shall afterwards endeavour to establish some comparisons with other countries, but with all the care and reserve which such comparisons require.

During the four years preceding 1830, 28,686 accused persons were set down as appearing before the courts of assize, that is to say, 7171 individuals annually nearly; which gives 1 accused person to 4463 inhabitants, taking the population at 32,000,000 souls. Moreover, of 100 accused, 61 persons have been condemned to punishments of greater or less severity. From the remarks made above with respect to the crimes which remain unknown or unpunished, and from mistakes which justice may make, we conceive that these numbers, although they furnish us with curious data for the past, do not give us any thing exact on the propensity to crime. However, if we consider that the two ratios which we have calculated have not sensibly varied from year to year, we shall be led to believe that they will not vary in a sensible manner for the succeeding years; and the probability that this variation will not take place is so much the greater, according as, all things being equal, the mean results of each year do not differ much from the general average, and these results have been taken from a great number of years. After these remarks, it becomes very probable that, for a Frenchman, there is 1 against 4462 chances that he will be an accused person during the course of the year; moreover, there are 61 to 39 chances, very nearly, that he will be condemned at the time that he is accused.

Thus, although we do not yet know the statistical documents for 1830, it is very probable that we shall again have 1 accused person in 4463 very nearly, and 61 condemned in 100 accused persons; this probability is somewhat diminished for the year 1831, and still more for the succeeding years. We may, therefore, by the results of the past, estimate what will be realised in the future. This possibility of assigning beforehand the number of accused and condemned persons which any country will present, must give rise to serious reflections, since it concerns the fate of several thousand men, who are driven, as it were, in an irresistible manner, towards the tribunals, and the condemnations which await them.

These conclusions are deduced from the principle, already called in so frequently in this work, that effects are proportionate to their causes, and that the effects remain the same, if the causes which have produced them do not vary. If France, then, in the year 1830, had not undergone any apparent change, and if, contrary to my expectation, I found a sensible difference between the two ratios calculated beforehand for this year and the real ratios observed, I should conclude that some alteration had taken place in the causes, which had escaped my attention. On the other hand, if the state of France had changed, and if, consequently, the causes which influence the propensity to crime have also undergone some change, I ought to expect to find an alteration in the two ratios which until that time remained nearly the same.

It is proper to observe, that the preceding numbers only show, strictly speaking, the probability of being accused and afterwards condemned, without rendering us able to determine any thing very precise on the degree of the propensity to crime; at least unless we admit, what is very likely, that justice preserves the same activity, and the number of guilty persons who escape it preserves the same proportion from year to year.

OF THE INFLUENCE OF KNOWLEDGE, OF PROFESSIONS,
AND OF CLIMATE, ON THE PROPENSITY TO CRIME

It may be interesting to examine the influence of the intellectual state of the accused on the nature of crimes: the French documents on this subject are such, that I am enabled to form the following table for the years 1828 and 1829; to this table I have annexed the results of the years 1830 and 1831, which were not known when the reflections which succeed were written down.

Thus, all things being equal, the number of crimes against persons, *compared with the number of crimes against property*, during the years 1828 and 1829, was greater according as the intellectual state of the accused was more highly developed; and this difference bore especially on murders, rapes, assassinations, blows, wounds, and other severe crimes. Must we thence conclude that knowledge is injurious to society? I am far from thinking so. To establish such an assertion, it would be necessary to commence by ascertaining how many individuals of the French nation belong to each of the four divisions which we have made above, and to find out if, proportion being considered, the individuals of that one of the divisions commit as many crimes as those of the others. If this were really the case, I should not hesitate to say that, since the most enlightened individuals commit as many crimes as those who have had less education, and since their crimes are more serious, they are necessarily more criminal; but from the little we know of the diffusion of knowledge in France, we cannot state any thing decisively on this point. Indeed, it may so happen, that individuals of the enlightened part of society, while committing fewer murders, assassinations, and other severe crimes, than individuals who have received no education, also commit much fewer crimes against property, and this would explain what we have remarked in the preceding numbers. This conjecture even becomes probable, when we consider that the enlightened classes are presupposed to possess more affluence, and consequently are less frequently under the necessity of having recourse

Intellectual state of the Persons Accused	1828–1829: Accused of Crimes against		Ratio of Crimes against Property to Crimes against Persons	1830–1831: Accused of Crimes against		Ratio of Crimes against Property to Crime against Persons
	Persons	Property		Persons	Property	
Could not read or write	2072	6,617	3·2	2134	6,785	3·1
Could read and write but imperfectly	1001	2,804	2·8	1033	2,840	2·8
Could read and write well	400	1,100	2·8	408	1,047	2·6
Had received a superior education to this 1st degree	80	206	2·6	135	184	1·4
	3553	10,736	3·0 aver.	3710	10,856	2·9 aver.

to the different modes of theft, of which crimes against property almost entirely consist; whilst affluence and knowledge have not an equal power in subduing the fire of the passions and sentiments of hatred and vengeance. It must be remarked, on the other hand, that the results contained in the preceding table only belong to two years, and consequently present a smaller probability of expressing what really is the case, especially those results connected with the most enlightened class, and which are based on very small numbers. It seems to me, then, that at the most we can only say that the ratio of the number of crimes against persons to the number of crimes against property varies with the degree of knowledge; and generally, for 100 crimes against persons, we may reckon fewer crimes against property, according as the individuals belong to a class of greater or less enlightenment.

ON THE INFLUENCE OF CLIMATE ON THE PROPENSITY TO CRIME

I shall remark that certain ratios cannot be rigorously compared, on account of the defective valuation (or census) of the population, or from an unequal degree of repression in the different courts of justice. It will be difficult enough to find out the errors arising from the first cause, as we have only, for the elements of verification, the relative numbers of births and deaths; as to the unequal degree of repression, such is not exactly the case, for, besides that we are led to believe that the activity of justice in finding out the authors of crimes is not every where the same, we see that acquittals are not always in the same ratio. Thus, according to the documents from 1825 to 1829, 61 individuals out of every 100 accused have been condemned in France, yet the degree of repression has generally been stronger in the northern than in the southern part of the country. The Court of Justice of Rouen has condemned the greatest number, and it has condemned 71 individuals out of 100 accused at the least; the courts of Dijon, Anjou, Douai, Nanci, Orleans, Caen, Paris, Rennes, have also excceded the average; the courts of Metz, Colmar, Amiens, Bordeaux, Bourges, Besançon, Grenoble, Lyons, and La Corse, have presented nearly the same average as France; whilst the acquittals have been more numerous in the southern courts, such as Toulouse, Poitiers, Nismes, Aix, Riom, Pau, Argen, Limoges, and Montpellier—the two last courts having condemned, at an average, only 52 individuals of 100 accused. It yet remains for examination, whether these decisive inequalities in the number of acquittals in the north and south of France are owing to a greater facility in bringing forward accusations, or to indulgence to the accused. It appears to me probable, that it may be in part owing to crimes against persons being more common, all things being equal, in the south, and crimes against property in the north; we know, also, that more acquittals take place in the first class of crimes than in the second. However the case may be, I think it will be proper not to lose sight of this double cause of error which I have just pointed out.

If we now cast our eyes over the departments of France which have exceeded the average of crimes against persons as well as of crimes against property, we shall first find Corsica and Landes to be, from their manners and customs, in peculiar circumstances, and which will scarcely permit of their being compared with the rest of France.

The Corsicans, indeed, impelled by cruel prejudices, and warmly embracing feelings of revenge, which are frequently transmitted from generation to generation, almost make a virtue of homicide, and commit the crime to excess. Offences against property are not frequent, and yet their number exceeds the average of France. We cannot attribute this state of things to want of instruction, since the number of accused who could neither read nor write was comparatively less than in France. This is not the case in Landes, where almost nine-tenths of the accused were in a state of complete ignorance. This department, where a poor and weak population live dispersed, as it were, in the midst of fogs, is one where civilisation has made the least progress. Although Landes is found in the most unfavourable class as regards crimes, it is nevertheless proper to say that it does not differ much from the average of France: we may make the same observations on the departments of Vienne and Ille-et-Vilaine. As to the other departments, we may observe that they are generally the most populous in France, in which we find four of the most important cities, Paris, Lyons, Marseilles, and Rouen; and that they also are the most industrious—those which present the greatest changes and intercourse with strangers. We may be surprised not to find with them the departments of the Gironde and Loire-Inférieure, which seem to be almost in the same circumstances as the departments of Bouches-du-Rhône and Seine-Inférieure, especially if we consider that, with respect to knowledge, they seem less favoured than these last, and the repression of crime also has generally been effective. This remark is particularly applicable to the department of the Gironde, for the Loire-Inférieure does not differ so much from the average of France. I shall not hesitate to attribute these differences to a greater morality in one part than the other. And this conjecture becomes more probable, if we observe that the whole of the departments of the south of France, which are on the shores of the sea from the Basses-Pyrénées to La Manche, except Landes and Ille-et-Vilaine which have already been mentioned, fall below the average of France for crimes against persons; and that, on the contrary, all the departments, without exception, which are on the shores of the Mediterranean, as well as the ones adjacent to them, exceed this average.

The following is a summary of what has been said:—

1. The greatest number of crimes against persons and property take place in the departments which are crossed by or near to the Rhone, the Rhine, and the Seine, at least in their navigable portions.

2. The fewest crimes against persons and property are committed in the departments in the centre of France, in those which are situated in the west towards the Atlantic, from the Basses-Pyrénées to La Manche, and in those towards the north, which are traversed by the Somme, the Oise, and the Meuse.

3. The shores of the Mediterranean and the adjacent departments show, all things being equal, a stronger propensity to crimes against persons, and the northern parts of France to crimes against property.

After having established these facts, if we seek to go back to the causes which produce them, we are immediately stopped by numerous obstacles. And, indeed, the causes influencing crimes are so numerous and different, that it becomes almost impossible to assign to each its degree of importance. It also frequently happens, that causes which appear very influential, disappear before others of which we had scarcely thought at first, and this is what I have especially found in actual researches: and I confess that I have been probably too much occupied with the influence which we assign to education in abating the propensity to crime; it seems to me that this common error especially proceeds from our expecting to find fewer crimes in a country, because we find more children in it who attend school, and because there is in general a greater number of persons able to read and write. We ought rather to take notice of the degree of moral instruction; for very often the education received at school only facilitates the commission of crime. We also consider poverty as generally conducing to crime; yet the department of Creuse, one of the poorest in France, is that which in every respect presents the greatest morality. Likewise, in the Low Countries, the most moral province is Luxembourg, where there is the greatest degree of poverty. It is proper, however, that we come to a right understanding of the meaning of the word poverty, which is here employed in an acceptance which may be considered improper. A province, indeed, is not poor because it possesses fewer riches than another, if its inhabitants, as in Luxembourg, are sober and active; if, by their labour, they can certainly obtain the means of relieving their wants, and gratifying tastes which are proportionally moderate; according as the inequality of fortune is less felt, and does not so much excite temptation: we should say, with more reason, that this province enjoys a moderate affluence. Poverty is felt the most in provinces where great riches have been amassed, as in Flanders, Holland, the department of the Seine, &c., and above all, in the manufacturing countries, where, by the least political commotion, by the least obstruction to the outlets of merchandise, thousands of individuals pass suddenly from a state of comfort to one of misery. These rapid changes from one state to another give rise to crime, particularly if those who suffer are surrounded by materials of temptation, and are irritated by the continual aspect of luxury and of the inequality of fortune, which renders them desperate.

ON THE INFLUENCE OF SEASONS ON THE PROPENSITY TO CRIME

The seasons have a well-marked influence in augmenting and diminishing the number of crimes. [T]he epoch of maximum (June) in respect to the number of crimes against persons, coincides pretty nearly with the epoch of minimum in respect to crimes against property, and this takes place in summer; whilst, on the contrary, the minimum of the number of crimes against persons, and the maximum of the number of crimes against property, takes place in winter. Comparing these two kinds of crimes, we find that in the month of January nearly four crimes take place against property to one against persons, and in the month of June only two to three. These differences are readily explained by considering that during winter misery and want are more especially felt, and cause an increase of the number of crimes against property, whilst the violence of the passions predominating in summer, excites to more frequent personal collisions.

ON THE INFLUENCE OF SEX ON THE PROPENSITY TO CRIME

We have already been considering the influence which climate, the degree of education, differences of the human race, seasons, &c., have on the propensity to crime; we shall now investigate the influence of sex.

At the commencement, we may observe that, out of 28,686 accused, who have appeared before the courts in France, during the four years before 1830, there were found 5416 women, and 23,270 men, that is to say, 23 women to 100 men. Thus, the propensity to crime in general gives the ratio of 23 to 100 for the sexes. This estimate supposes that justice exercises its duties as actively with regard to women as to men; and this is rendered probable by the fact, that the severity of repression is nearly the same in the case of both sexes; in other words, that women are treated with much the same severity as men.

We have just seen that, in general, the propensity to crime in men is about four times as great as in women, in France; but it will be important to examine further, if men are four times as criminal, which will be supposing that the crimes committed by the sexes are equally serious. We shall commence by making a distinction between crimes against property and crimes against persons. At the same time, we shall take the numbers obtained for each year, that we may see the limits in which they are comprised:—

Years	Crimes against Persons			Crimes against Property		
	Men	Women	Ratio	Men	Women	Ratio
1826	1639	268	0·16	4073	1008	0·25
1827	1637	274	0·17	4020	998	0·25
1828	1576	270	0·17	4396	1156	0·26
1829	1552	239	0·15	4379	1203	0·27
Averages	1601	263	0·16	4217	1091	0·26
1830	1412	254	0·18	4196	1100	0·26
1831	1813	233	0·13	4567	993	0·22
Averages	1612	243	0·15	4381	1046	0·24

Although the number of crimes against persons may have diminished slightly, whilst crimes against property have become rather more numerous, yet we see that the variations are not very great; they have but little modified the ratios between the numbers of the accused of the two sexes. We have 26 women to 100 men in the accusations for crimes against property, and for crimes against persons the ratio has been only 16 to 100. In general, crimes against persons are of a more serious nature than those against property, so that our distinction is favourable to the women, and we may affirm that men, in France, are four times as criminal as women. It must be observed, that the ratio 16 to 26 is nearly the same as that of the strength of the two sexes. However, it is proper to examine things more narrowly, and especially to take notice of individual crimes, at least of those which are committed in so great a number, that the inferences drawn from them may possess some degree of probability. For this purpose, in the following table I have collected the numbers relating to the four years before 1830, and calculated the different ratios; the crimes are classed according to the degree of magnitude of this ratio. I have also grouped crimes nearly of the same nature together, such as issuing false money, counterfeits, falsehoods in statements or in commercial transactions, &c.

Nature of Crimes	Men	Women	Women to 100 Men
Infanticide	30	426	1320
Miscarriage	15	39	260
Poisoning	77	73	91
House robbery (*vol domestique*)	2648	1602	60
Parricide	44	22	50
Incendiarism of buildings and other things	279	94	34
Robbery of churches	176	47	27
Wounding of parents (*blessures envers ascendans*)	292	63	22
Theft	10,677	2249	21
False evidence and suborning	307	51	17
Fraudulent bankruptcy	353	57	16
Assassination	947	111	12
False coining (*fousse monnaie*), counterfeit making, false affirmations in deeds, &c.	1669	177	11
Rebellion	612	60	10
Highway robbery	648	54	8
Wounds and blows	1447	78	5
Murder	1112	44	4
Violation and seduction	685	7	1
Violation on persons under 15 years of age	585	5	1

As we have already observed, to the commission of crime the three following conditions are essential—the will, which depends on the person's morality, the opportunity, and the facility of effecting it. Now, the reason why females have less propensity to crime than males, is accounted for by their being more under the influence of sentiments of shame and modesty, as far as morals are concerned; their dependent state, and retired habits, as far as occasion or opportunity is concerned; and their physical weakness, so far as the facility of acting is concerned. I think we may attribute the differences observed in the degree of criminality to these three principal causes. Sometimes the whole three concur at the same time: we ought, on such occasions, to expect to find their influence very marked, as in rapes and seductions; thus, we have only 1 woman to 100 men in crimes of this nature. In poisoning, on the contrary, the number of accusations for either sex is nearly equal. When force becomes necessary for the destruction of a person, the number of women who are accused becomes much fewer; and their numbers diminish in proportion, according to the necessity of the greater publicity before the crime can be perpetrated: the following crimes also take place in the order in which they are stated—infanticide, miscarriage, parricide, wounding of parents, assassinations, wounds and blows, murder.

With respect to infanticide, woman has not only many more opportunities of committing it than man, but she is in some measure impelled to it, frequently by misery, and almost always from the desire of concealing a fault, and avoiding the shame or scorn of society, which, in such cases, thinks less unfavourably of man. Such is not the case with other crimes involving the destruction of an individual: it is not the degree of the crime which keeps a woman back, since, in the series which we have given, parricides and wounding of parents are more numerous than assassinations, which again are more frequent than murder, and wounds and blows generally; it is not simply weakness, for then the ratio for parricide and wounding of parents should be the same as for murder and wounding of strangers. These differences are more especially owing to the habits and sedentary life of females; they can only conceive and execute guilty projects on individuals with whom they are in the greatest intimacy: thus, compared with man, her assassinations are more often in her family than out of it; and in society she commits assassination rather than murder, which often takes place after excess of drink, and the quarrels to which women are less exposed.

If we now consider the different kinds of theft, we shall find that the ratios of the propensity to crime are arranged in a similar series: thus, we have successively house robbery, robbery in churches, robberies in general, and, lastly, highway robbery, for which strength and audacity are necessary. The less conspicuous propensity to cheating in general, and to fraudulent bankruptcy, again depend on the more secluded life of females, their separation from trade, and that, in some cases, they are less capable than men—for example, in coining false money and issuing counterfeits.

OF THE INFLUENCE OF AGE ON THE PROPENSITY TO CRIME

Of all the causes which influence the development of the propensity to crime, or which diminish that propensity, age is unquestionably the most energetic. Indeed, it is through age that the physical powers and passions of man are developed, and their energy afterwards decreases with age. Reason is developed with age, and continues to acquire power even when strength and passion have passed their greatest vigour. Considering only these three elements, strength, passion, and judgment (or reason), we may almost say, *à priori,* what will be the degree of the propensity to crime at different ages. Indeed, the propensity must be almost nothing at the two extremes of life; since, on the one hand, strength and passion, two powerful instruments of crime, have scarcely begun to exist, and, on the other hand, their energy, nearly extinguished, is still further deadened by the influence of reason. On the contrary, the propensity to crime should be at its maximum at the age when strength and passion have attained their maximum, and when reason has not acquired sufficient power to govern their combined influence. Therefore, considering only physical causes, the propensity to crime at different ages will be a property and sequence of the three quantities we have just named, and might be determined by them, if they were sufficiently known. But since these elements are not yet determined, we must confine ourselves to seeking for the degrees of the propensity to crime in an experimental manner; we shall find the means of so doing in the *Comptes Généraux de la Justice*. The following table will show the number of crimes against persons and against property, which have been committed in France by each sex during the years 1826, 27, 28, and 29, as well as the ratio of these numbers; the fourth column points out how a population of 10,000 souls is divided in France, according to age; and the last column gives the ratio of the total number of crimes to the corresponding number of the preceding column; thus there is no longer an inequality of number of the individuals of different ages.

Individuals' Age	Crimes against Persons	Crimes against Property	Crimes against Property in 100	Population according to Age	Degrees of the Propensity to Crime
Less than 16 years	80	440	85	3304	161
16 to 21 years	904	3723	80	887	5217
21 to 25	1278	3329	72	673	6846
25 to 30	1575	3702	70	791	6671
30 to 35	1153	2883	71	732	5514
35 to 40	650	2076	76	672	4057
40 to 45	575	1724	75	612	3757
45 to 50	445	1275	74	549	3133
50 to 55	288	811	74	482	2280
55 to 60	168	500	75	410	1629
60 to 65	157	385	71	330	1642
65 to 70	91	184	70	247	1113
70 to 80	64	137	68	255	788
80 and upwards	5	14	74	55	345

This table gives us results conformable to those which I have given in my *Recherches Statistique* for the years 1826 and 1827. Since the value obtained for 80 years of age and upwards is based on very small numbers, it is not entitled to much confidence. Moreover, we see that man begins to exercise his propensity to crimes against property at a period antecedent to his pursuit of other crimes. Between his 25th and 30th year, when his powers are developed, he inclines more to crimes against persons. It is near the age of 25 years that the propensity to crime reaches its maximum; but before passing to other considerations, let us examine what difference there is between the sexes. The latter columns of the following table show the degrees of propensity to crime, reference being had to population, and the greatest number of each column being taken as unity:—

Individuals' Age	Accused Men	Accused Women	Women to 1000 Men	Degrees of the Propensity to Crime In General	Men	Women	Calculated
Under 16 years	438	82	187	0·02	0·02	0·02	0·02
16 to 21	3,901	726	186	0·76	0·79	0·64	0·66
21 to 25	3,762	845	225	1·00	1·00	0·98	1·00
25 to 30	4,260	1017	239	0·97	0·96	1·00	0·92
30 to 35	3,254	782	240	0·81	0·80	0·83	0·81
35 to 40	2,105	621	295	0·59	0·56	0·75	0·71
40 to 45	1,831	468	256	0·55	0·54	0·60	0·60
45 to 50	1,357	363	267	0·46	0·44	0·51	0·51
50 to 55	896	203	227	0·33	0·33	0·33	0·42
55 to 60	555	113	204	0·24	0·24	0·22	0·34
60 to 65	445	97	218	0·24	0·24	0·23	0·27
65 to 70	230	45	196	0·16	0·17	0·14	0·21
70 to 80	163	38	233	0·12	0·12	0·12	0·12
80 & upwards	18	1	56	0·05	0·06	0·01	0·04
All ages	23,270	5416	233	0·41	—	—	—

Women, compared to men, are rather later in entering on the career of crime, and also sooner come to the close of it. The maximum for men takes place about the 25th year, and about the 30th for women; the numbers on which our conclusions are founded are still very few; yet we see that the two lines which represent the relative value for each sex are almost parallel.

From the data of the preceding tables, it is scarcely possible not to perceive the great influence which age exercises over the propensity to crime, since each of the individual results tend to prove it. I shall not hesitate to consider the scale of the different degrees of the propensity to crime, at different ages, deserving of as much confidence as those which I have given for the stature, weight, and strength of man, or, finally, those for mortality.

CONCLUSIONS

In making a summary of the principal observations contained in this chapter, we are led to the following conclusions:—

1st, Age (or the term of life) is undoubtedly the cause which operates with most energy in developing or subduing the propensity to crime.

2d, This fatal propensity appears to be developed in proportion to the intensity of the physical power and passions of man: it attains its maximum about the age of 25 years, the period at which the physical development has almost ceased. The intellectual and moral development, which operates more slowly, subsequently weakens the propensity to crime, which, still later, diminishes from the feeble state of the physical powers and passions.

3d, Although it is near the age of 25 that the maximum in number of crimes of different kinds takes place, yet this maximum advances or recedes some years for certain crimes, according to the quicker or slower development of certain qualities which have a bearing on those crimes. Thus, man, driven by the violence of his passions, at first commits violation and seduction; almost at the same time he enters on the career of theft, which he seems to follow as if by instinct till the end of life; the development of his strength subsequently leads him to commit every act of violence—homicide, rebellion, highway robbery; still later, reflection converts murder into assassination and poisoning. Lastly, man, advancing in the career of crime, substitutes a greater degree of cunning for violence, and becomes more of a forger than at any other period of life.

4th, The *difference of sexes* has also a great influence on the propensity to crime: in general, there is only 1 woman before the courts to 4 men.

5th, The propensity to crime increases and decreases nearly in the same degree in each sex; yet the period of maximum takes place rather later in women, and is near the 30th year.

6th, Woman, undoubtedly from her feeling of weakness, rather commits crimes against property than persons; and when she seeks to destroy her kind, she prefers poison. Moreover, when she commits homicide, she does not appear to be proportionally arrested by the enormity of crimes which, in point of frequency, take place in the following order:—infanticide, miscarriage, parricide, wounding of parents, assassination, wounds and blows, murder; so that we may affirm that the number of the guilty diminishes in proportion as they have to seek their victim more openly. These differences are no doubt owing to the habits and sedentary life of woman; she can only conceive and execute guilty projects on individuals with whom she is in constant relation.

7th, The *seasons,* in their course, exercise a very marked influence on crime: thus, during summer, the greatest number of crimes against persons are committed, and the fewest against property; the contrary takes place during winter.

8th, It must be observed that age and the seasons have almost the same influence in increasing or diminishing the number of mental disorders and crimes against persons.

9th, *Climate* appears to have some influence, especially on the propensity to crimes against persons: this observation is confirmed at least among the races of southern climates, such as the Pelasgian race, scattered over the shores of the Mediterranean and Corsica, on the one hand; and the Italians, mixed with Dalmatians and Tyrolese, on the other. We observe, also, that severe climates, which give rise to the greatest number of wants, also give rise to the greatest number of crimes against property.

10th, The countries where frequent mixture of the people takes place; those in which industry and trade collect many persons and things together, and possess the greatest activity; finally, those where the inequality of fortune is most felt, all things being equal, are those which give rise to the greatest number of crimes.

11th, Professions have great influence on the nature of crimes. Individuals of more independent professions are rather given to crimes against persons; and the labouring and domestic classes to crimes against property. Habits of dependence, sedentary life, and also physical weakness in women, produce the same results.

12th, *Education* is far from having so much influence on the propensity to crime as is generally supposed. Moreover, moral instruction is very often confounded with instruction in reading and writing alone, and which is most frequently an accessory instrument to crime.

13th, It is the same with *poverty*; several of the departments of France, considered to be the poorest, are at the same time the most moral. Man is not driven to crime because he is poor, but more generally because he passes rapidly from a state of comfort to one of misery, and an inadequacy to supply the artificial wants which he has created.

14th, The higher we go in the ranks of society, and consequently in the degrees of education, we find a smaller and smaller proportion of guilty women to men; descending to the lowest orders, the habits of both sexes resemble each other more and more.

15th, Of 1129 murders committed in France, during the space of four years, 446 have been in consequence of quarrels and contentions in taverns; which would tend to show the fatal influence of the use of *strong drinks*.

16th, In France, as in the Low Countries, we enumerate annually 1 accused person to 4300 inhabitants nearly; but in the former country, 39 in 100 are acquitted, and in the second only 15; yet the same code was used in both countries, but in the Low Countries the judges performed the duty of the jury. Before correctional courts and simple police courts, where the committed were tried by judges only, the results were nearly the same for both countries.

17th, In France, crimes against persons were about one-third of the number of crimes against property, but in the Low Countries they were about one-fourth only. It must be remarked, that the first kind of crimes lead to fewer condemnations than the second, perhaps because there is a greater repugnance to apply punishment as the punishment increases in severity.

I cannot conclude this chapter without again expressing my astonishment at the constancy observed in the results which the documents connected with the administration of justice present each year.

"Thus, as I have already had occasion to repeat several times, we pass from one year to another, with the sad perspective of seeing the same crimes reproduced in the same order, and bringing with them the same punishments in the same proportions." All observations tend likewise to confirm the truth of this proposition, which I long ago announced, that *every thing which pertains to the human species considered as a whole, belongs to the order of physical facts*; the greater the number of individuals, the more does the influence of individual will disappear, leaving predominance to a series of general facts, dependent on causes by which society exists and is preserved. These causes we now want to ascertain, and as soon as we are acquainted with them, we shall determine their influence on society, just in the same way as we determine effects by their causes in physical sciences. It must be confessed, that, distressing as the truth at first appears, if we submit to a well followed out series of observations of the physical world and the social system, it would be difficult to decide in respect to which of the two the acting causes produce their effects with most regularity. I am, however, far from concluding that man can do nothing for man's amelioration. I think, as I said at the commencement of this work, that he possesses a moral power capable of modifying the laws which affect him; but this power only acts in the slowest manner, so that the causes influencing the social system cannot undergo any sudden alteration; as they have acted for a series of years, so will they continue to act in time to come, until they can be modified. Also, I cannot repeat too often, to all men who sincerely desire the well-being and honour of their kind, and who would blush to consider a few francs more or less paid to the treasury as equivalent to a few heads more or less submitted to the axe of the executioner, that there is a budget which we pay with a frightful regularity—it is that of prisons, chains, and the scaffold: it is that which, above all, we ought to endeavour to abate.

HENRY MAYHEW
(1812–1887)

Dickens' phrase "It was the best of times. It was the worst of times." could not more accurately describe Victorian London. It was the best of times and places if you were rich—the worst if poor. It was of the poor that Henry Mayhew became the foremost chronicler.

Born one of a large number of children of Joshua Dorset Joseph Mayhew, a solicitor, Henry attended the Westminister School at twenty. There he soon showed a stubborn independence which was to characterize the remainder of his life by having to leave school after three years for reading his Greek lessons during chapel. He later took a minor position in his father's law firm but had to abandon that as well when, on one occasion, he subjected his father to contempt proceedings for neglecting to deliver certain papers to court on time.

He next set his hand to writing, and produced a few mediocre plays and other literary trivia. His writing career improved somewhat when he and a friend brought out the journal, Figero in London *in 1831.* During Mayhew's editorship, the paper engaged in fair but acerbic commentary on public affairs and especially in exposing corruption in government and quasi-governmental agencies. But as with most of Mayhew's ventures, this was not to endure. After the demise of Figero in London, he engaged in other equally profitless schemes for making money—including an attempt to manufacture diamonds chemically.

Mayhew then began a project for which he is probably only slightly less well known than for his monumental London Labor and the London Poor. *He became one of the four who founded* Punch. *His editorship of this magazine, though relatively brief, was of decisive importance; and the strong element of iconoclasm which characterized it from the beginning showed the persistence of Mayhew's earlier efforts on* Figero in London.

London Labor and the London Poor *began as a series of articles for the newspaper,* The Morning Chronicle. *Starting with a piece entitled "A Visit to the Cholera Districts of Bermondsey," Mayhew provided increasing detail of the growing masses who lived in the backwash of Victorian capitalism. Interrupted at times by journalistic interference and by a lawsuit, all of the articles and other writings which exposed London's teeming underworld were finished in 1862, gathered into four volumes, and published in their final form. They provided one of the most fundamental of socio-historical documents and one of the finest examples of literate social protest.*

The selections which follow are taken from the fourth volume of London Labor and the London Poor *and describe a portion of "Those who Will Not Work." Regrettably, space allows only a modest selection from that volume, that devoted exclusively to the subject of thieves. Mayhew also described the lives of the various types of swindlers, prostitutes, and beggars. It should be noted that the same depth of pathos found with the poor in other volumes of* London Labor and the London Poor *may not be quite as evident in his discussion of theft. However much one may deplore it on moral grounds, the thief has made what may be for him a rational, energetic, and manly response to his poverty; an adjustment denied those who still remain wedged between penury and moral scruple.*

HENRY MAYHEW

London Labor and the London Poor

THIEVES AND SWINDLERS

In tracing the geography of a river it is interesting to go to its source, possibly a tiny spring in the cleft of a rock in some mountain glen. You follow its windings, observing each tributary which flows into its gathering flood until it discharges its waters into the sea. We proceed in a similar manner to treat of the thieves and swindlers of the metropolis.

Thousands of our felons are trained from their infancy in the bosom of crime; a large proportion of them are born in the homes of habitual thieves and other persons of bad character, and are familiarized with vice from their earliest years; frequently the first words they lisp are oaths and curses. Many of them are often carried to the beershop or gin palace on the breast of worthless drunken mothers, while others, clothed in rags, run at their heels or hang by the skirts of their petticoats. In their wretched abodes they soon learn to be deceitful and artful, and are in many cases very precocious. The greater number are never sent to school; some run idle about the streets in low neighbourhoods: others are sent out to beg throughout the city; others go out with their mothers and sit beside their stalls; while others sell a handful of matches or small wares in our public thoroughfares.

One day, in going down a dark alley in the Borough, near Horsemonger Lane Gaol, we saw a little boy—an Irish cockney, who had been tempted to steal by other boys he was in the habit of associating with. He was stripped entirely naked, and was looking over a window on the first floor with a curious grin on his countenance. His mother had kept his clothes from him that day as a punishment for stealing, and to prevent him getting out of the house while she went out to her street-stall.

In our brief sketch of the criminals of the metropolis, we have in the outset directed our attention to the sneaks or common thieves—by far the larger number of our criminal population—from whose ranks the expert pickpockets and the ingenious and daring burglars in most cases emerge. We have treated of the incipient stage of thieving, when the child of five or six years of age steals an apple or an orange, or a handful of nuts from a stall, or an old pair of boots from a shop door, and then traced the after-stages of more daring crime.

There are thousands of neglected children loitering about the low neighbourhoods of the metropolis, and prowling about the streets, begging and stealing for their daily bread. They are to be found in Westminster, Whitechapel, Shoreditch, St. Giles's, New Cut, Lambeth, the Borough, and other localities. Hundreds of them may be seen leaving their parents' homes and low lodging-houses every morning sallying forth in search of food and plunder. They are fluttering in rags and in the most motley attire. Some are orphans and have no one to care for them; others have left their homes and live in lodging-houses in the most improvident manner, never thinking of to-morrow; others are sent out by their unprincipled parents to beg and steal for a livelihood; others are the children of poor but honest and industrious people, who have been led to steal through the bad companionship of juvenile thieves. Many of them have never been at a day-school nor attended a Sunday or ragged-school, and have had no moral or religious instruction. On the contrary, they have been surrounded by the most baneful and degrading influences, and have been set a bad example by their parents and others with whom they came in contact, and are shunned by the honest and industrious classes of society. The chief agencies which have tended to ameliorate their condition are the ragged-schools, where they receive sound secular and religious instruction; the shoeblacks' brigades, where they are trained in habits of honest industry; and the juvenile reformatories, which have been instituted for their moral and social elevation.

Many of them are hungry, and have no food to eat nor money to purchase it, and readily steal when they find a suitable opportunity. Not having received the benefit of a sound moral training, they have not the conscientious scruples possessed by the children of honest parents; their only care is to avoid being detected in their felonies. When they successfully steal some article from a stall or shop-door, or rifle a till by entering the shop, they are congratulated on their expertness by their companions, and enjoy a larger share of plunder.

The public streets of the metropolis are regarded by these ragged little felons and the children of honest industrious parents in a very different aspect. The latter walk the streets with their eyes sparkling with wonder and delight at the beautiful and grand sights of the metropolis. They are struck with the splendour of the shops and the elegance and stateliness of the public buildings, and with the dense crowds of people of various orders, and trains of vehicles thronging the streets. These little ragged thieves walk along the streets with very different emotions. They, too, in their own way, enjoy the sights and sounds of London. Amid the busy crowds many of them are to be seen sitting in groups on the pavement or loitering about in good-humour and merriment; yet ever and anon their keen roguish eyes sparkle as they look into the windows of the confectioners', bakers', and greengrocers' shops, at the same time keeping a sharp eye on the policeman as he passes on his beat.

These juvenile thieves find an ample field for plunder at the stalls and shop-doors in Whitechapel, Shoreditch, Edgeware Road, and similar localities, where many articles are exposed for sale, which can be easily disposed of to some of the low fences. In this manner thousands of our felons are trained to be expert and daring in crime, and are frequently tried and convicted before the Police Courts.

This is the main source of the habitual felons of the metropolis. As these boys and girls grow up they commence a system of sneaking thefts over the metropolis, some purloining in shops, others gliding into areas and lobbies on various pretences, stealing articles from the kitchen, and when opportunity occurs carrying off the plate.

As these young felons advance in years they branch off into three different classes, determined partly by their natural disposition and personal qualities, and partly by the circumstances in which they are placed. Many of them continue through life to sneak as common thieves, others become expert pickpockets, and some ultimately figure as burglars.

A vast number of juvenile thieves as they grow up continue to carry on a system of petty felonies over the metropolis, and reside in the lowest neighbourhoods. Some pretend to sell laces and small wares to get a pretext to call at the houses of labouring people and tradesmen, and to go down the areas and enter the lobbies in fashionable streets. In addition to the paltry profits arising from these sales they get a livelihood by begging, and as a matter of course do not scruple to steal when they can find an opportunity.

These common thieves are of both sexes, and of various ages, and are often characterized by mental imbecility and low cunning. Many of them are lazy in disposition and lack energy both of body and mind. They go out daily in vast shoals over the metropolis picking up a miserable and precarious livelihood, sometimes committing felonies in the houses they visit of considerable value.

The pickpockets are of various ages and of different degrees of proficiency, from the little ragged urchin in St. Giles's stealing a handkerchief at the tail of a gentleman's coat, to the elegantly dressed and expert pickpocket promenading in the West-end and attending fashionable assemblies. Some are dressed as mechanics, others as clerks, some as smart business men, and others in fashionable attire. They are to be found on all public occasions, some of them clumsy and timid, others daring and most expert. Many of them continue to pursue this class of felonies in preference to any other. They receive a considerable accession to their numbers by young women, frequently servants who have been seduced, and cohabit with burglars, pickpockets, and others, and who are trained to this infamous profession, and in many cases are shoplifters.

Many are trained to commit housebreaking and burglaries from fourteen to fifteen years of age. Boys are occasionally employed to enter through fanlights and windows, and to assist otherwise in plundering dwellings and shops. Some of them commit burglaries of small value in working neighbourhoods, where comparatively little ingenuity and skill are required, others plunder shops and warehouses and fashionable dwellings, which is generally done with greater care and ingenuity, and where the booty is often of higher value.

In addition to the three classes we have named, the common thief, the pickpocket, and the burglar, there is another class of low ruffians who frequently cohabit with low women and prostitutes, and commit highway robberies. They often follow these degraded females on the streets, and attack persons who accost them, believing them to be prostitutes. At other times they garotte men on the street at midnight, or in the by-streets in the evening, and plunder them with violence. This class of persons are generally hardened in crime, and many of them are returned convicts.

The habitual crime of the female portion of the community is in most cases associated with prostitution. We learn from statistics collected by the metropolitan constabulary for 1860, that there are nearly 7000 open prostitutes or street-walkers in London, three fourths of whom we have reason to believe are addicted to stealing. While many of these belong to our native-born felon population, a large proportion have been seduced from the ranks of honest and industrious people in

London, or have come up from the provinces, while a few of them are from the Continent.

We believe that the most effective means of checking the crime of the metropolis is to have an efficient machinery of ragged schools in those low neighbourhoods, where neglected children are to be found, similar to the ragged school in George's Yard, and to train them in honest employment, as in the shoeblack brigades or industrial schools.

We learn from the statistics of the constabulary of the metropolis that juvenile crime has been considerably reduced within the past ten years. Several of our police inspectors have laboured with untiring industry to reform the lodging-houses and to introduce cleanliness and decency, where immorality and filth formerly prevailed. And noble exertions have been made by Christian societies to illumine these dark localities with the light of Christian truth.

Yet much still remains to be done. And it is a problem worthy of our highest and wisest statesmen to consider whether adequate means to elevate this abandoned class are to be provided by voluntary effort, or by the paternal care of our Government from the public treasury.

It is far easier to train the young in virtuous and industrious habits, than to reform the grown-up felon who has become callous in crime, and it is besides far more profitable to the State. To neglect them or inadequately to attend to their welfare gives encouragement to the growth of this dangerous class. On the other hand how noble the aim, to adopt wise and vigorous measures to provide for these children of adversity and misfortune, and to transform them into useful members of society!

Our national reformatories are very useful in reclaiming those juveniles who have fallen into crime; but ragged schools efficiently conducted would be of still higher value—as prevention is better than cure. In providing those noble machineries by voluntary effort, or by the State, we would wisely act as the minister of Divine Providence, and would thereby promote the best interests and prosperity of our country.

THE SNEAKS, OR COMMON THIEVES

The common thief is not distinguished for manual dexterity and accomplishment, like the pickpocket or mobsman, nor for courage, ingenuity, and skill, like the burglar, but is characterized by low cunning and stealth—hence he is termed the *Sneak,* and is despised by the higher classes of thieves.

There are various orders of Sneaks—from the urchin stealing an apple at a stall, to the man who enters a dwelling by the area or an attic window and carries off the silver plate.

In treating of the various classes of common thieves and their different modes of felony, we shall first treat of the juvenile thieves and their delinquencies, and notice the other classes in their order, according to the progressive nature and aggravation of their crime.

Street-stalls. In wandering along Whitechapel we see ranges of stalls on both sides of the street, extending from the neighbourhood of the Minorities to Whitechapel church. Various kinds of merchandize are exposed to sale. There are stalls for fruit, vegetables, and oysters. There are also stalls where fancy goods are exposed for sale—combs, brushes, chimney-ornaments, children's toys, and common articles of jewellery. We find middle-aged women standing with baskets of firewood, and Cheap Johns selling various kinds of Sheffield cutlery, stationery, and plated goods.

It is an interesting sight to saunter along the New Cut, Lambeth, and to observe the street stalls of that locality. Here you see some old Irish woman, with apples and pears exposed on a small board placed on the top of a barrel, while she is seated on an upturned bushel basket smoking her pipe.

Alongside you notice a deal board on the top of a tressel, and an Irish girl of 18 years of age seated on a small three-legged stool, shouting in shrill tones "Apples, fine apples, ha'penny a lot!"

You find another stall on the top of two tressels, with a larger quantity of apples and pears, kept by a woman who sits by with a child at her breast.

In another place you see a costermonger's barrow, with large green and yellow piles of fruit of better quality than the others, and a group of boys and girls assembled around him as he smartly disposes of pennyworths to the persons passing along the street.

Outside a public-house you see a young man, humpbacked, with a basket of herrings and haddocks standing on the pavement, calling "Yarmouth herrings—three a-penny!" and at the door of a beershop with the sign of the "Pear Tree" we find a miserable looking old woman selling cresses, seated on a stool with her feet in an old basket.

As we wander along the New Cut during the day, we do not see so many young thieves loitering about; but in the evening when the lamps are lit, they steal forth from their haunts, with keen roguish eye, looking out for booty. We then see them loitering about the stalls or mingling among the throng of people in the street, looking wistfully on the tempting fruit displayed on the stalls.

These young Arabs of the city have a very strange and motley appearance. Many of them are only 6 or 7 years of age, others 8 or 10. Some have no jacket, cap, or shoes, and wander about London with their ragged trowsers hung by one brace; some have an old tattered coat, much too large for them, without shoes and stockings, and with one leg of the trowsers rolled up to the knee; others have on an old greasy grey or black cap, with an old jacket rent at the elbows, and strips of the lining hanging down behind; others have on an old dirty pinafore; while some have petticoats. They are generally in a squalid and unwashed condition, with their hair clustered in wild disorder like a mop, or hanging down in dishevelled locks,—in some cases cropped close to the head.

Groups of these ragged urchins may be seen standing at the corners of the streets and in public thoroughfares, with blacking-boxes slung on their back by a leathern belt, or crouching in groups on the pavement; or we may occasionally see them running alongside of omnibuses, cabs, and hansoms, nimbly turning somersaults on the pavement as they scamper along, and occasionally walking on their hands with their feet in the air in our fashionable streets, to the merriment of the passers-by. Most of them are Irish cockneys, which we can observe in their features and accent—to which class most of the London thieves belong. They are generally very acute and ready-witted, and have a knowing twinkle in their eye which exhibits the precocity of their minds.

As we ramble along the New Cut in the dusk, mingled in the throng on the crowded street, chiefly composed of working people, the young ragged thieves may be seen stealing forth: their keen eye readily recognizes the police-officers proceeding in their rounds, as well as the detective officers in their quiet and cautious movements. They seldom steal from costermongers, but frequently from the old women's stalls. One will push an old woman off her seat—perhaps a bushel basket, while the others will steal her fruit or the few coppers lying on her stall. This is done by day as well as by night, but chiefly in the dusk of the evening.

They generally go in a party of three or four, sometimes as many as eight together. Watching their opportunity, they make a sudden snatch at the apples or pears, or oranges or nuts, or walnuts, as the case may be, then run off, with the cry of "stop thief!" ringing in their ears from the passers-by. These petty thefts are often done from a love of mischief rather than from a desire for plunder.

When overtaken by a police-officer, they in general readily go with him to the police-station. Sometimes the urchin will lie down in the street and cry "let me go!" and the bystanders will take his part. This is of frequent occurrence in the neighbourhood of the New-cut and the Waterloo-road—a well-known rookery of young thieves in London.

In the Mile-end-road, and New North-road, and occasionally in other streets in different localities of London, common jewellery is exposed for sale, consisting of brooches, rings, bracelets, breast-pins, watch-chains, eye-glasses, ear-rings and studs, &c. There are also stalls for the sale of china, looking-glasses, combs, and chimney-ornaments. The thefts from these are generally managed in this way:—

One goes up and looks at some trifling article in company with his associates. The party in charge of the stall—generally a woman—knowing their thieving propensity, tells them to go away; which they decline to do. When the woman goes to remove him, another boy darts forward at the other end of the stall and steals some article of jewellery, or otherwise, while her attention is thus distracted.

Stealing from the Tills. This is done by the same class of boys, generally by two or three, or more, associated together. It is committed at any hour of the day, principally in the evening, and generally in the following way: One of the boys throws his cap into the shop of some green-grocer or other small dealer, in the absence of the person in charge; another boy, often without shoes or stockings, creeps in on his hands and knees as if to fetch it, being possibly covered from without by some of the boys standing beside the shop-door, who is also on the look-out. Any passerby seeing the cap thrown in would take no particular notice in most cases, as it merely appears to be a thoughtless boyish frolic. Meantime the young rogue within the shop crawls round the counter to the till, and rifles its contents.

Stealing from the Doors and Windows of Shops. In various shopping districts of London we see a great variety of goods displayed for sale at the different shop-doors and windows, and on the pavement in front of the shops of brokers, butchers, grocers, milliners, &c.

Let us take a picture from the New-cut, Lambeth. We observe many brokers' shops along the street, with a heterogenous assortment of household furniture, tables, chairs, looking-glasses, plain and ornamental, cupboards, fire-screens, &c., ranged along the broad pavement; while on tables are stores of carpenters' tools in great variety, copper-kettles, brushes, and bright tin pannikins, and other articles.

We see the dealer standing before his door, with blue apron, hailing the passer-by to make a purchase. Upon stands on the pavement at each side of his shop-door are cheeses of various kinds and of different qualities, cut up into quarters and slices, and rashers of bacon lying in piles in the open windows, or laid out on marble slabs. On deal racks are boxes of eggs, "fresh from the country," and white as snow, and large pieces of bacon, ticketed as of "fine flavour," and "very mild."

Alongside is a milliner's shop with the milliner, a smart young woman, seated knitting beneath an awning in front of her door. On iron and wooden rods, suspended on each side of the door-way, are black and white straw bonnets and crinolines, swinging in the wind; while on the tables in front are exposed boxes of gay feathers, and flowers of every tint, and fronts of shirts of various styles, with stacks of gown-pieces of various patterns.

A green-grocer stands by his shop with a young girl of 17 by his side. On each side of the door are baskets of apples, with large boxes of onions and peas. Cabbages are heaped at the front of the shop, with piles of white turnips and red carrots.

Over the street is a furniture wareroom. Beneath the canvas awning before the shop are chairs of various kinds, straw-bottomed and seated with green or puce-coloured leather, fancy looking-glasses in gilt frames, parrots in cages, a brass-mounted portmanteau, and other miscellaneous articles. An active young shopman is seated by the shop-door, in a light cap and dark apron—with newspaper in hand.

Near the Victoria Theatre we notice a second-hand clothes store. On iron rods suspended over the doorway we find trowsers, vests, and coats of all patterns and sizes, and of every quality dangling in the wind; and on small wooden stands along the pavement are jackets and coats of various descriptions. Here are corduroy jackets, ticketed "15s. and 16s. made to order." Corduroy trowsers warranted "first rate," at 7s. 6d. Fustian trowsers to order for 8s. 6d.; while dummies are ranged on the pavement with coats buttoned upon them, inviting us to enter the shop.

In the vicinity we see stalls of workmen's iron tools of various kinds— some old and rusty, others bright and new.

Thefts are often committed from the doors and windows of these shops during the day, in the temporary absence of the person in charge. They are often seen by passers-by, who take no notice, not wishing to attend the police court, as they consider they are insufficiently paid for it.

The coat is usually stolen from the dummy in this way: one boy is posted on the opposite side of the street to see if a police-officer is in sight, or a policeman in plain clothes, who might detect the depredation. Another stands two or three yards from the shop. The third comes up to the dummy, and pretends to look at the quality of the coat to throw off the suspicion of any bystander or passer-by. He then unfastens the button, and if the shop-keeper or any of his assistants come out, he walks away. If he finds that he is not seen by the people in the shop, he takes the coat off the dummy and runs away with it.

If seen, he will not return at that time, but watches some other convenient opportunity. When the young thief is chased by the shop-keeper, his two associates run and jostle him, and try to trip him up, so as to give their companion an opportunity of escaping. This is generally done at dusk, in the winter time, when thieving is most prevalent in those localities.

In stealing a piece of bacon from the shop-doors or windows, they wait till the shopman turns his back, when they take a piece of bacon or cheese in the same way as in the case alluded to. This is commonly done by two or more boys in company.

Handkerchiefs at shop-doors are generally stolen by one of the boys and passed to another who runs off with it. When hotly chased, they drop the handkerchief and run away.

Another class of Sneaks, who steal from the outside of shops, are women more advanced in life—some middle-aged and others elderly. Some of them are thieves, or the companions of thieves, and others are the wives of honest, hard-working mechanics and labouring men, who spend their money in gin and beer at various public-houses.

These persons go and look over some pieces of bacon or meat outside of butchers' shops; they ask the price of it, sometimes buy a small piece and steal a large one, but more frequently buy none. They watch the opportunity of taking a large piece which they slip into their basket and carry to some small chandler's shop in a low neighbourhood, where they dispose of it at about a fourth of its value.

We have met some thieves of this order, basket in hand, returning from Drury Lane, who were pointed out to us by a detective officer.

The mechanics' and labourers' wives in many cases leave their homes in the morning for the purpose of purchasing their husband's dinner. They meet with other women fond of drink like themselves. They meet, for example, outside the "Plumb Tree," or such-like public-house, and join their money together to buy beer or gin. After partaking of it, they leave the house, and remain for some time outside conversing together. They again join their money and return to the public-house, and have some additional liquor: leave the house and separate. Some of them join with other parties fond of liquor as they did with the former. One says to the other: "I have no money, otherwise we would have a drop of gin. I have just met Mrs. So-and-so, and spent nearly all my money." The other may reply: "I have not much to get the old man's dinner, but we can have a quartern of gin." After getting the liquor, they separate. The tradesman's wife, finding that she has spent nearly the whole of her money, goes to a cheese-monger's or butcher's shop, and steals a piece of meat, or bacon, for the purpose of placing it before her husband for dinner, perhaps selling the remainder of the booty at shops in low neighbourhoods, or to lodging-houses.

Such cases frequently occur, and are brought before the police-courts.

These persons sometimes steal flat-irons for ironing clothes at the brokers' shop-doors, which they carry to other pawnbrokers if not detected. At other times they take them to the leaving-shop of an unlicensed pawnbroker. On depositing them, they get a small sum of money. These leaving-shops are in the lowest localities, and take in articles pawnbrokers would refuse. They are open on Sundays, and at other times when no business is done in pawnbrokers' shops.

These shops are well known to the police, and give great assistance to these Sneaks in disposing of their stolen property.

Small articles are occasionally taken from shop windows in the winter evenings, by means of breaking a pane of glass in a very ingenious way. These thefts are committed at the shops of confectioners, tobacconists, and watchmakers, &c., in the quiet by-streets.

Sometimes they are done by the younger ragged-boys, but in most cases by lads of 14 and upwards, belonging to the fraternity of London thieves.

In the dark winter evenings we may sometimes see groups of these ragged boys, assembled around the windows of a small grocery-shop, looking greedily at the almond-rock, lollipops, sugar-candy, barley-sugar, brandy-balls, pies, and tarts, displayed in all their tempting sweetness and in all their gaudy tints. They insert the point of a knife or other sharp instrument into the corner or side of the pane, then give it a wrench, when the pane cracks in a semicircular starlike form around the part punctured. Should a piece of glass large enough to admit the hand not be sufficiently loosened, they apply the sharp instrument at another place in the pane, when the new cracks communicate with the rents already made; on applying a sticking-plaster to the pane, the piece readily adheres to it, and is abstracted. The thief inserts his hand through an opening in the window, seizes a handful of sweets or other goods, and runs away, perhaps followed by the shopman in full chase. These thieves are termed star-glazers.

Such petty robberies are often committed by elder lads at the windows of tobacconists, when cigars and pipes are frequently stolen.

They cut the pane in the manner described, and sometimes get a younger boy to commit the theft, while they get the chief share of the plunder, without having exposed themselves to the danger of being arrested stealing the property.

Stealing from Children. Children are occasionally sent out by their mothers, with bundles of washing to convey to different persons, or they may be employed to bring clothes from the mangle. They are sometimes met by a man, at other times by a woman, who entices them to go to a shop for a halfpenny or a penny worth of sweets, meanwhile taking care they leave their parcels or bundle, which they promise to keep for them till they return. On their coming out of the shop, they find the party has decamped, and seldom any clue can be got of them, as they may belong to distant localities of the metropolis.

In other cases they go up to the children, when they are proceeding on their way, with a bundle or basket, and say: "You are going to take these things home. Do you know where you are going to take them?" The child being taken off her guard may say she is "carrying them to Mrs. So-and-so, of such a street." They will then say, "You are a good girl, and are quite right. Mrs. So-and-so sent me for them, as she is in a hurry and is going out." The child probably gives her the basket or bundle, when the thief absconds. A case of this kind occurred in the district of Marylebone about six months ago.

A girl was going with two silk-dresses to a lady in Devonshire-street, when she was met by a young woman, who said she was a servant of the lady, and was sent to get the dresses done or undone, and was very glad she had met her. The woman was an entire stranger to the lady. The larceny was detected on the Saturday night, and the lady was put to great inconvenience, as she had not a dress to go out with on the Sunday. Robberies of clothes sent out to be mangled, and of articles of linen are very common. Milliners often send young girls errands who are not old enough to see through the tricks of these parties prowling about the metropolis.

These larcenies are generally committed by vagrants decently dressed, and too lazy to work, who go sneaking about the streets and live in low neighbourhoods, such as St. Giles's, Drury-lane, Short's-gardens, Queen-street, and the Borough. They are in most cases committed in the evening, though sometimes during the day.

Stealing from Drunken Persons. There is a very common low class of male thieves, who go prowling about at all times of the day and night for this purpose.

They loiter about the streets and public-houses to steal from drunken persons, and are called "Bug-hunters" and "mutchers." You see many of them lounging about gin-palaces in the vicinity of the Borough, near St. George's church. We have met them there in the course of our rambles over the metropolis, and at Whitechapel and St. Giles's. They also frequent the Westminster-road, the vicinity of the Victoria Theatre, Shoreditch, and Somers Town. These low wretches are of all ages, and many of them have the appearance of bricklayers', stone-masons', and engineers' labourers. They pretend they are labourers out of work, and are forward in intruding themselves on the notice of persons entering those houses, and expect to be treated to liquor, though entire strangers to them.

They are not unfrequently so rude as to take the pewter-pot of another person from the bar, and pass it round to their comrades, till they have emptied the contents. If remonstrated with, they return insulting language, and try to involve the person in a broil.

You occasionally find them loafing about the tap-rooms. They watch for drunken people, whom they endeavour to persuade to treat them. They entice him to go down some court or slum, where they strip him of his watch, money, or other valuables he may have on his person. Or they sometimes rob him in the public-house; but this seldom occurs, as they are aware it would lead to detection. They prefer following him out of the public-house. Many of these robberies are committed in the public urinals at a late hour at night.

These men have often abandoned women who cohabit with them, and assist them in these low depredations. They frequently dwell in low courts and alleys in the neighbourhood of gin-palaces, have no settled mode of life, and follow no industrious calling—living as loafers and low ruffians.

There is another class of thieves, who steal from drunken persons, usually in the dusk of the evening, in the following manner: Two women, respectably dressed, meet a drunken man in the street, stop him and ask him to treat them. They adjourn to the bar of a public-house for the purpose of getting some gin or ale. While drinking at the bar, one of the women tries to rob him of his watch or money. A man who is called a "stickman," an accomplice and possibly a paramour of hers, comes to the bar a short time after them. He has a glass of some kind of liquor, and stands beside them. Some motions and signs pass between the two females and this man. If they have by this time secured the booty, it is passed to the latter, who, thereupon slips away, with the stolen articles in his possession.

In some cases, when the property is taken from the drunken man, one of the women on some pretext steps to the door and passes it to the "stickman" standing outside, who then makes off with it. In other cases these robberies are perpetrated in the outside of the house, in some by-street.

Sometimes the man quickly discovers his loss, and makes an outcry against the women; when the "stickman" comes up and asks, "what is the matter?" the man may reply, "these two women have robbed me." The stickman answers "I'll go and fetch a policeman." The property is passed to him by the women, and he decamps. If a criminal information is brought against the females, the stolen goods are not found in their possession, and the case is dropped.

Robberies from Carts and other Vehicles. There are many depredations committed over the metropolis from carts, carriers' waggons, cabs, railway vans, and other vehicles. Many of those people have the appearance of porters at a warehouse, and are a peculiar order.

At one time they may have been porters at warehouses, or connected with railways, or carmen to large commercial firms. Some have corduroy or moleskin jacket and trowsers, and cloth cap; others have a plain frock-coat and cap.

Many of the robberies from carts are done by the connivance of the carters. They are sent by business establishments to dispose of goods over the metropolis; some of them are connected with the worst class of thieves. They connive with those men in stealing their employers' property, and in rifling other carts, carry the booty away in their own, and always manage to secure a part of the prize.

These carters take thieves occasionally to railway stations to assist them with their work, and when an opportunity occurs, carry off goods from the railway platform, such as bales of bacon, cheese, bags of nails, boxes of tin and copper, and travellers' luggage, which they dispose of to marine-store dealers and at chandlers' shops. The wearing apparel in the trunks they sell at second-hand shops, kept by Jews and others in low neighborhoods, such as Petticoat-lane, Lambeth, Westminster, and the Borough of Southwark.

Robberies by False Keys. There are many robberies committed in the metropolis by means of false keys, generally between the hours of seven and nine o'clock in the evening. After nine o'clock they would be considered burglaries. This class of robberies is generally committed by thieves of experience, and frequently, before depredations are committed, persons call at the house in the daytime, who take particular notice of the lock of the street-door, to know the key which opens it, whether a Bramah, Chubb, or other lock. These persons are termed "putters up of robberies," and supply the thieves with the requisite information, when they come in the evening and enter the house. In many cases they get clear off with the booty.

The houses entered are frequently respectable lodging-houses, or houses occupied by one family where there is likely to be no children about the upper rooms. In the case of entering these dwellings they make their way to the bed-rooms above, their chief object being to steal the jewellery and dressing-case left on the dressing-table, often of great value. They also take clothes out of the drawers, and other articles. On coming out they often put on some of the apparel, such as an overcoat, and fill the pockets with stolen property.

In houses in the West-end, single gentlemen, such as government clerks, officers in the army, and others, are often out dining in the evening, or at the clubs; and as the servant is generally engaged downstairs at this time, the thief is frequently not obstructed.

To elude suspicion from the police constables in the street they often have a carpet-bag to carry off the booty. If they meet one of them near the house, they generally ask him some question, such as the way to some street, to take him off his guard.

Robberies by Servants. There are a great number of felonies committed by servants over the metropolis, many of which might be prevented by prudent precautions on the part of their employers. On this subject we would wish to speak with discrimination. We are aware that many honest and nobleminded servants are treated with injustice by the caprice and bad temper of their employers, and many a poor girl is without cause dismissed from her situation, and refused a proper certificate of character. Being unable to get another place, she is often driven with reluctance from poverty and destitution to open prostitution on the street. On the other hand, many of our employers foolishly and thoughtlessly receive male and female servants into their service without making a proper inquiry into their previous character.

Many felonies are committed by domestic female servants who have been only a month or six weeks in service. Some of them steal tea, sugar, and other provisions, which are frequently given to acquaintances or relatives out of doors. Others occasionally abstract linen and articles of wearing-apparel, or plunder the wardrobe of gold bracelets, rings, pearl necklace, watch, chain, or other jewellery, or of muslin and silk dresses and mantles, which they either keep in their trunk, or otherwise dispose of.

Female domestic servants are often connected with many of the felonies committed in the metropolis. Two of the female servants in a gentleman's family are sometimes courted by two smart dressed young men, bedecked with jewellery, who visit them at the house occasionally. One of them may call by himself on a certain evening, and after sitting with them for some time in the kitchen, may pretend that he is going upstairs to the front door on some errand, such as to bring in some liquor. He goes alone, and opens the door to his companion whom he had arranged to meet him, and who may be hovering in the street. He admits him into the house to rifle the rooms in the floors above. Meantime he comes in with the liquor, and proceeds down stairs, and remains there for some time to occupy the attention of the servants until his companion has plundered the house of money, jewels, or other property.

On other occasions two young men may remain downstairs with the servants, while a third party is committing a robbery in the apartments above.

Some respectable-looking young women, in the service of middle-class and fashionable families, are connected with burglars, and have been recommended to their places through their influence, or that of their acquaintances. Some of these females are usually not a fortnight or a month in service before a heavy burglary is committed in the house, and will remain for two or three months longer to prevent suspicion. They will then take another similar place in a gentleman's family, remain several months there, and by their conduct ingratiate themselves into the good graces of the master and mistress, when another burglary is committed through their connivance. The booty is shared between them and the thieves.

Some continue this system for a considerable time, as their employers have no suspicion of their villainy. They are often Irish cockneys, connected with the thieves, and have been trained with them from their infancy. They generally aim at stealing the silver plate, clothes, and other valuables. In these robberies they are always ready to give the "hue and cry" when a depredation has been committed.

CESARE LOMBROSO
(1835–1909)

On a cold, grey, November morning—so the story goes—a brigand named Vilella breathed his last in an asylum in Pavia. A young physician on the staff was assigned to the post-mortem examination. As Lombroso later described it, he had laid open the skull and had begun to examine its contents when he discovered on that part of the occiput where a spine should be found in the normal individual a depression which he named the "median occipital fossa." This condition, he claimed, was correlated with hypertrophy of the vermis—an anomalous condition in man but often found in the lower apes, rodents, and birds.

> This was not merely an idea but a revelation. At the sight of that skull, I seemed to see all of a sudden, lighted up as a vast plain under a flaming sky the problem of the nature of the criminal—an atavistic being who reproduces in his person the ferocious instincts of primitive humanity and the inferior animals.

Cesare Lombroso, surely one of the best known, and possibly one of the least well understood figures in criminology, was born in Verona on November 6, 1835. He attended the Gymnasium, and by virtue of his having reviewed an historical work of Paulo Marzolo was encouraged by that famous physician to enter upon the study of medicine. He obtained degrees in medicine and surgery in 1858 and 1859.

During his medical studies he had become deeply interested in psychiatry and the anatomy of the brain, and for a time early in his career was in charge of a number of hospitals for the insane in various parts of Italy. In 1876 he received an appointment in legal medicine at the University of Turin. It was in the same year that Lombroso's interest in the criminal, an interest which had increasingly become the subject of some of his medical and psychiatric papers, shown forth in the form of a book: L'Uomo Delinquente. This work, Lombroso's best known, went through five Italian editions growing from a single volume of something in excess of two hundred pages to a massive three-volume work of almost two thousand pages—with an atlas added to *contain the photographs, diagrams, and charts which would not fit into the text proper.*

Lombroso married in 1869 and fathered two daughters, Paola and Gina, both of whom helped their father with his work at his home in Turin. All evidence suggests that Lombroso led an enviable life for a criminologist. His home was filled with books, his laboratory with the skulls of criminals, and his museum with prison memorabilia— all carefully stewarded by his daughters and the hosts of students come to pay homage to the "father of modern criminology." Among the latter was Enrico Ferri who was to contribute to Lombroso's later emphasis on sociology as Lombroso had contributed to his interest in the criminal. With Ferri and Raphael Garofalo he founded the Archives of Psychiatry and Criminal Anthropology *in 1880. In 1896, Lombroso was appointed Professor of Psychiatry at the University of Turin, and in 1906 Professor of Criminal Anthropology. In that year also he founded the Museum of Criminal Anthropology.*

Among the factors which may contribute to a misunderstanding of Lombroso, two are outstanding. First, his theories changed greatly from one period to another during his professional career. His concept of atavism which originally referred to a reversion to some sort of subhuman species came to be supplemented by explanations involving arrested development, degeneracy, and epilepsy. His entire approach to crime became more eclectic involving increased attention to a multitude of factors beyond the strictly clinical. This is shown in Lombroso's typology of offenders. In addition to "criminal man," or what Ferri came to call the "born criminal," Lombroso recognized the "insane criminal" and the "epilectic criminal." More importantly, however, he suggested the major class of "occasional criminals," which type is not characterized by atavism or degeneracy. This major class of "occasional criminals" includes "pseudo criminals," normal individuals who involuntarily commit petty offenses; "criminaloids," who may be abnormal to a degree but whose crime is committed by reason of overwhelming environmental factors; and, finally, the "habitual criminal" who commits crimes as the result of improper socialization. Surely these categories have counterparts—in some cases rather exact counterparts—in many of the typologies which succeed this one in criminological history.

Second, Lombroso represents a good deal more in criminology than his analytical theory alone would indicate. His methodology can be seen as the beginning of clinical criminology—a necessary and useful addition to the legalistic and statistical schools which preceded it. Moreover, the implications of the clinical position for penology—

clearly described by Lombroso—can be seen in the schools of "social defense" so popular in European criminology today.

One other cause of misunderstanding may be that L'Uomo Delinquente *has never been fully translated into English. There is a later work,* Crime its Causes and Remedies, *which as a whole is a fair summary in English of the author's final eclecticism. However, as an example of Lombroso's earlier formative statements, parts of several privately translated chapters of the first edition of* L'Uomo Delinquente *are presented here. These have been made available through the generosity and kind permission of Professor Leonard Savitz of Temple University.*

CESARE LOMBROSO

Criminal Man

THE ANATOMICAL EVIDENCE OF ATAVISM

I have thought it useful to begin the study of delinquents with an anatomical discussion which permits a complete detailed examination, although necessarily limited, of a relatively small number of individuals—66 in all.

Commencing with the most important study, that of cranial capacity of criminals, it is clear from the measurement of the circumference that a small number are of very large circumference (1 @ 580, 1 @ 550, 2 @ 560, and 2 @ 540 out of 65), the others of ordinary circumference (8 @ 530, 13 @ 520), and that there is also a rather remarkable number of circumferences which are almost microcephalic: 39 out of 65, namely 19 @ 510, 8 @ 490, and 12 @ 500.

As for the measured capacity in cubic centimeters, I am only perfectly certain about 40 males. Out of these 40, the average capacity is 1389 which, if compared with the normal average, works out to be clearly much lower. Generally, thieves show an even lower capacity (1321) compared with murderers (1415).

The facial angle only three times attained 80° and 81°, always in the case of murderers or brigand chiefs, all of whom had attained maximum cerebral capacity. In all the other 38, this, almost without distinction as to region, appears lower.

Cranial sutures were found to be normal only 17 times; 5 times they were still found to be open in old persons exceeding 75 and 80 years of age, and these were of men who had been famous in their criminal activities up to a late age. Some of these men had considerable cerebral capacity, but in others it was quite small, and accompanied by various pithecoid anomalies.

In 13 out of 56 cases, a median occipital depression was found. In 11 of these, it was of ordinary dimensions, but in one of these 13, a man from Bologna, this occipital depression was in the proportion of twice or more than the normal. Finally, in still another, Vilella of Calabria, a most skillful thief with cranial sutures still open at 70 years of age, this depression appeared to be of truly extraordinary proportions, 34 mm. long, 23 mm. wide, 11 mm. deep. It was associated with atrophy of the lateral occipital depressions, a complete absence of any internal occipital spine, of which it took the place, and was limited at the sides by two bony projections running at first parallel, thus giving it a trapezoidal appearance, while near the occipital orifice it ended in a slight bony promontory, triangular in shape. From such appearances, comparative anatomy and human embriology have solid reasons for deriving the induction that in this case there was undoubted hypertrophy of the vermis, a real tiny median brain. This would be highly uncharacteristic of adult primates, but would be more characteristic of the rodents and the lemurs, or even of man between the 3rd and 4th month after conception.

We found other elements of regression offered by the falling away of the forehead, and thus also by the encasement of the ethmoids in the orbital vaults. This is associated with reduction of the frontal lobes. Seven times among these 29, we found protrusion of the zygomatic apophysis of the frontal bone; 5 times out of 35, a depression of the nasal glabella was noticed. The Wormian bones, in 11 cases out of 66, were found to be in anomalous positions.

If we look at these data as a whole, and compare them with those for mad persons (excluding cretins and idiots), we find with not a little surprise that the cranial deviations of the criminals are almost as numerous and perhaps even more numerous than those of the mad persons.

One or two other features, such in particular as those median occipital depressions of Vilella, already mentioned; the dual articular face of the occipital condyle; flattening of the palate; encasement of the ethmoid in the nasal channel; the low value of the cephalospinal index and orbital index; and the exaggerated prognathism—all these might lead us to an even more remote preatavism. However, we cannot explain thereby the frequent obliquity of the cranium and the face; or the fusion, or the welding over of the atlas with the occiput; or the permanence of the frontal sutures at an advanced age; or the plagiocephalia. These facts would seem to point to an error in the foetal cranial development, which cannot have failed to exercise considerable influence on the development of the intelligence, and therefore on the morals of the individual.

These deviations are not found in isolation, but almost always are grouped in a number of individuals who present a collection of deviations. Thus in the case of Vilella, we found not only synosteosis and atrophy of the atlas, but atrophy of the lateral occipital depressions, hypertrophy of the median, obliquity of the cranium, etc.

Is it possible that individuals accumulating such an enormous series of deviations would have the same degree of intelligence, and the same sense of responsibility as men with perfectly normal crania? It should be noted that these cranial deviations only express the coarsest of the lesions of the intellectual centre, deviations in the volume and the shape. What would happen if it were possible to collect histological data or perhaps even only to examine the macroscopic details of their brains?

To many it will have seemed a reckless, vain task on my part to draw any conclusions from the few measurements carried out on corpses regarding the cranial forms of delinquent man. This might have been so had I not had the good fortune to be able to check this small number against some 832 other measurements taken on living persons.

The stature of delinquents, for example, almost always reproduces the regional type. But comparing these results with those for the average of persons who are healthy, provided by figures for conscripts, we find that in almost all the Italian regions the stature of delinquents is greater than the average.

This superiority, which is in contradiction to what is known from the studies of Thompson and Wilson, would appear to depend especially on the large number of highwaymen and homicides, who provide the smallest number of low statures compared with the ravishers, forgers, and particularly the robbers, in respect of all of whom we were only able to collect rather scanty details compared with the former.

As regards weight, if we compare the results obtained by comparing the weight of 1331 soldiers, with the average weight of delinquents, we find an appreciable increase in weight among delinquents. This accords with what we have already discovered regarding statures.

If we proceed now to study separately only the cranial circumference as the measurement which can best be compared with that of healthy persons, we see in general that the maximum among delinquents is found in the case of the forgers, the highwaymen, and the homicides;

and the minimum in the case of the fire-raisers, the thieves, and the ravishers.

To appreciate the differences between these measurements and those of healthy persons, we will compare them with the results obtained from 14,000 soldiers and from 262 lunatics. We then find that there are three times as many voluminous heads among healthy persons as among delinquents; and delinquents show sub-microcephalia almost twice as frequently as soldiers, though less often, than in the case of lunatics.

The majority of persons hold very erroneous opinions regarding the physiognomy of delinquents. The novelists make of them men of frightening aspect, with beards up to their very eyes, with scintillating, ferocious eyes and aquiline noses. Some more serious observers go to the opposite extreme and find no difference between them and normal persons.

Both are wrong.

Certainly, just as there are delinquents with remarkable cranial capacities and most beautiful formations of the cranium, so there are also, principally among the skillful swindlers and also among bandit chiefs, some with perfectly regular physiognomies.

But these are exceptions, striking and fascinating by the contrast they present to our expectations, and explained by the fact that these are almost always persons of uncommon intelligence combined frequently with a certain gracefulness of form.

But when, instead of these isolated individuals, these rare examples forming the oligarchy of crime, we come to study the whole mass of these unfortunate wretches, as fell to my lot in the various houses of correction, we find that, without having always a physiognomy which is grim or frightful, they yet have one which is quite peculiar to them, and almost special for each form of delinquency. It is precisely some of these features of their physiognomy, such for example as the absence of any beard, or an abundance of hair, which have led to our finding their faces more gentle and delicate than they really are.

Generally, robbers have considerable mobility of the face and hands; small, shifting, quick-moving eyes; bushy, connecting eyebrows; twisted or snub noses, thin beards, a head of hair which is not always dense, and foreheads almost receding. Both they and the ravishers frequently have the earlap inserted almost like a handle on the head.

In the case of the ravishers, on the other hand, the eyes are almost always shining, and they have a delicate physiognomy, with swollen lips and eyelids. Otherwise, they are frail and sometimes hunch-backed.

Male prostitutes are frequently distinguished by a feminine elegance of the hair and clothes which they preserve even in prison uniform.

Habitual homicides have glassy, cold, motionless eyes, sometimes bloodshot and injected. The nose is often aquiline, or rather hawk-like, and always voluminous. The jaws are strong, and the zygomata are wide. The hair is frizzy, dense, and dark. Very frequently the beard is scanty. The canine teeth are well-developed, and the lips thin. There is frequently nystagmus and unilateral contraction of the face, the teeth being revealed and the jaws contracted.

Morbidity of the skin, an infantile appearance, and an abundance of smooth, almost effeminate hair, I have found to be present in almost all fire-raisers, one of whom, a most curious individual, from Pesaro, was known as the "woman" and really had the habits and appearance of a woman.

The few forgers I have been able to study had small eyes, fixed on the ground, twisted noses, frequently long and voluminous, and not infrequently premature whitening of the hair or baldness.

In general, all delinquents have handle-like ears, an abundance of hair, scanty beards, conspicuous frontal depressions, protruding chins, widened zygomata and frequent gesticulations.

The custom of many of our brigands of wearing pigtails, and that of cut-throats of wearing a forelock as the hallmark of their ferocious trade, are both probably attributable to a particular abundance of curly, unruly hair around the parting.

But anthropology calls for figures and not isolated descriptions of a general nature, particularly when it is to be applied to forensic medicine; and it will therefore be useful to present in subsequent pages those I succeeded in collecting, not indeed on 800, but on 390 delinquents from Emilia, the Marche, and Southern Italy.

THE ATAVISM OF CRIME AND PUNISHMENT

After reading this book, the reader will perhaps be convinced that many of the characteristics found in savages and among the coloured races are also to be found in habitual delinquents. They have in common, for example, thinning hair, lack of strength and weight, low cranial capacity, receding foreheads, highly developed frontal sinuses, a high frequency of medio-frontal sutures, precocious synosteosis (especially frontal), protrusion of the curved line of the temporal, simplicity of the sutures, considerable thickness of the cranial bone, enormous development of the jaws and the zygomata, obliquity of the orbits, darker skin, thicker, curly hair, large, or handle-shaped ears, a greater analogy between the two sexes, less pronounced genetic activity, a lower degree of sensitivity to pain, complete moral insensitiveness, indolence, the absence of any remorse, improvidence appearing at times in the guise of courage, and courage alternating with base cowardice, great vanity, facile superstition, exaggerated susceptibility of the ego, and finally the relative concept of the divinity and morals.

Analogies extend to minor details, e.g., an abundance of metaphor and onomatopoeia in speech, improvised laws within associations, the peculiarly personal influence of their chiefs, the custom of tatooing, the same special literature recalling that of heroic times (as they were called by Vico) when crime was extolled and for preference thought tended to take on a rhythmical, rhymed form.

This atavism explains the nature and distribution of certain crimes. It would be difficult to explain pederasty, and infanticide, which gain a hold over entire associations, if we were to overlook the times of the Romans and the Greeks when not only were these acts not considered crimes, but even sometimes seen as customary behavior. This perhaps suggests an explanation for the frequent association of aesthetic tastes among pederasts, just as was the case with the Greeks.

Pushing the atavistic analogy still further, even beyond race, we can explain certain other phenomena of the criminal world which would otherwise appear to be inexplicable, even to the expert in psychiatry. For example, the frequency of the welding over of the atlas with the occiput is repeated in certain fossilised cetacea. The median occipital depression and its extraordinary development is found in the Lemurs and the Rodents. The tendency towards cannibalism, even without feelings of vendetta, and even more, that form of sanguinary ferocity mixed with lust, as shown by Gille, Verzeni, Legier, Bertrand, Artusio, and the Marquis de Sade, recalls the time when copulation in man, as in the case of animals, was preceded by and associated with fierce and bloody struggles, both to subdue the resistance of the female and also to conquer rivals in love. In many tribes in Australia, the lover is accustomed to waiting for his wife behind a hedge, knocking her unconscious with a blow from his club and carrying her senseless into the marital house. Traces of these customs remain in the nuptial rites in many of our valleys, and in the horrible feasts of the Jagraate and in the Roman bacchanals where anyone, including males, offering any resistance to rape was cut into such small pieces that the corpse could not be found.

The first and greatest writer on nature, Lucretius, had observed how even in the most ordinary cases of mating there may be found a germ of savagery against the woman, spurring us on to injure anyone hindering our satisfaction. I know of an eminent poet who no sooner sees a calf shot or even its bleeding carcass hanging, is seized with lust; and another who experiences ejaculations merely strangling a fowl or a pigeon. Mantegazza heard the confessions of a friend who, being about to kill a number of fowl, after the first killing experienced savage joy as he avidly fingered the hot, steaming entrails, and who from this fury was assailed by an attack of lechery.

These facts clearly prove that the most horrific crimes, and those which are most inhuman, still have a point of departure which is physiological and atavistic. This is to be found in those animal instincts which, held in check for a time in man by his upbringing, his surroundings, and his fear of punishment, suddenly break out under the influence of circumstances, such as sickness, atmospheric phenomena, imitation, or spermatic inebriation as a result of excessive continence (as found in early puberty, in paretics, uncivilised persons, or those compelled to lead a celibate or solitary existence, e.g., priests, shepherds, and soldiers).

Since it is known that certain disease conditions such as head injuries, meningitis, alcoholism and other forms of chronic intoxication and certain physiological conditions such as old age cause development of the nervous centres to halt and consequently produce atavistic regression, we can appreciate how they must facilitate the tendency towards crime.

Knowing that the delinquent is not far removed from the uncouth and the savage, and that at times the distance between them disappears altogether, we can appreciate why men from the lower orders, even if not immoral, so frequently have a real predilection for crime and why convicts in turn mix so easily with savages, adopting their customs entirely, including their cannibalism, as happens in Australia and Guyana.

Observing how our children, before they are educated, being unable to distinguish between vice and virtue, steal, fight, and lie without the least compunction, we can understand why so many abandoned children, orphans, and foundlings give way to evil habits.

Atavism also assists us in understanding the ineffectiveness of punishment and the strange fact of the constant, periodic recurrence of a given number of crimes. The greatest variations shown by the number of crimes against the person did not exceed one-twentyfifth and in the case of those against property one-fiftieth. In equal proportions we find for given months predominating a given group of crimes, e.g., lechery in July and June, poisoning and vagrancy in May, theft and forgery in January, thus depending on given variations in the thermometer or the cost of food. We find, Maury observes rather aptly, that we are governed by silent laws, but ones which never fall into disuse, governing society more surely than the laws contained in the statutes.

In short, crime would appear, both from statistics and from anthropological investigation, to be a natural phenomenon; some philosophers would even say a necessary phenomenon, like birth, death, and conception.

This idea of the necessity of crime, presumptuous though it may appear, is neither a new conception nor so very unorthodox, as many might think at first sight. Many years ago it was propounded by Casaubono when he wrote: "Man does not sin, but is dominated in varying degrees"; and by Plato who attributed the perversity of the criminal to his organisation and education, to the point of making his masters and parents responsible for him. St. Bernard has stated: "Who is there among us, however expert, who can distinguish in his impulses the influence of the serpent's sting from that of the sick mind." St. Augustine manifested this sentiment even more clearly when he wrote that even the angels could not bring it about that a man loving evil should instead love goodness.

Indirectly then it is affirmed by all the authors, even those of the most opposing systems who, when they venture on the terrain of facts, including that most elastic terrain of definitions, contradict themselves or their colleagues and fail to reach any conclusion whatsoever.

If we compare the various endeavours by the statutes, we find that the legislator never succeeds in fixing the theory of irresponsibility and finding a precise definition for it. All agree as to what is a good or a bad action, but it is difficult if not impossible to distinguish "whether the depraved act was committed with a full or incomplete consciousness of the evil" wrote Mittermayer. May, in his *Penal Legislation*, 1851, writes: "We still have no scientific knowledge of responsibility." E. Mahring, in *The Future of Penal Legislation*, states: "The question of irresponsibility is one which criminal justice cannot solve in any special case with certainty"; and indeed there are men who suffer from incipient madness or have such a disposition thereto that they can fall into it at the slightest encouragement, while others, owing to heredity, are impelled to peculiar behaviour and to immoral excesses. Awareness of the nature of a crime, says Delbruk, even with an investigation of the body and the mind of the criminal before and after the crime, is insufficient to solve the question of responsibility. Instead we need to know the life of the criminal, beginning with the cradle and ending with the anatomical table. But post-mortems cannot be undertaken on the criminal while he is still alive.

Carrara admits that there may be "absolute imputability where there is a consensus of intellect and will in the commission of a criminal act"; but he immediately adds "provided this is not diminished by the intervention of physical, intellectual and moral causes." But we have seen that there is no crime in which these causes are absent.

Again Pessina, while he states that "he who wills and executes a crime must answer for it before the justice, and the act of willing does not permit of intrinsic graduations" goes on to add that these graduations are only admissible when there is a greater or lesser freedom to elect owing to age, sex, ignorance, insanity, passionate exaltation or error of fact. And these are circumstances which are found present in one or other of all crimes.

Buccellati writes: "In the present state of knowledge, it is no exaggeration to state that complete imputability is strictly speaking, for all practical purposes, impossible."

Here it will be asked: "But if you deny imputability, what right have you to punish? You say he is irresponsible and then you punish him. What lack of logic and what hardness!" And I cannot forget how a venerable thinker, shaking his head as he read these pages, said to me: "Where are you arriving with these premises? Perhaps we should allow ourselves to be robbed and killed by gangs since it is doubtful whether they know they are doing wrong?" My reply is as follows: There is nothing less logical than that which tries to be too much so; there is nothing more imprudent than trying to derive from theories, even those which are soundest, conclusions which might cause even the smallest social upheaval. Just as a doctor at his patient's bedside, however certain of a given system, must have his doubts when serious danger is involved.

The scientific determination of the causes of crime is not at odds with a doctrine of imputability as a matter of social policy. There is need for science in the analysis of crime, but there is need for it in defence and punishment as well. Punishment will thus acquire a much less savage character, but also one which is less contradictory, and certainly more effective.

I do not believe there is any theory on the right to punish which would stand firmly on its base, once that is removed which refers to natural necessity, the right of self-defence, the old Italian theory of Beccaria and Romagnosi, of Garmignani and in part of Rosmini, Manini and Ellero. These, as far as I am aware, had their champion in Poletti who went so far, even before these studies appeared, as to wish to change the right to punish into penal tutelage.

We find this theory in Germany propounded by Hommel, Feuerbach, by Grollmann and Holtzendorf, in England by Hobbes and Bentham and in France by Ortolan.

In France there is a royal procurator who declares: "Man has no right to punish; for that, he would require to possess absolute knowledge and justice." Were it not in the name of the most absolute necessity, how could man arrogate to himself the right to judge his fellows? Otherwise, from the fact that man could not defend himself without inflicting punishment, the conclusion might be drawn that he had the right to inflict it. The very proof of his weakness is quoted in witness of his virtue. But that there is no such virtue is seen from the fact that, no sooner the alleged right becomes removed from the fact, it loses all its value.

Moreover, what better demonstration is there than that provided by the law of grace? It is exercised, it is customary to say, to temper justice when it is too severe; but if so, how can it be said to be just? A woman, forsaken by her lover and pregnant, alone and starving, conceived the idea of making forged banknotes which were grotesque and were immediately recognisable: she was sentenced to 5 years but handed over, since she was probably mad, to the mercy of the sovereign. But I say: If she were mad, she ought not to have been sentenced; and if she were not mad, she ought not to have been pardoned.

It is moreover so true that this law is entirely founded on fact, with nothing which of itself is absolute, that we find it varying from judge to judge depending on his sympathies and his customs. One judge, being used to dealing with major criminals in the Appeal Courts, will inflict relatively more severe punishment even for minor offences, passing sentences in months instead of in days. And moreover, there are no judges in the same country who agree exactly as to the sentence, even when an identical crime is involved.

And in any event, who will not see in this defensive concept a kind of right which we exercise at all times during our lives?

Someone may ask whether wild beasts tear men apart owing to their depraved malevolence or as a reaction of their own organism, but there will hardly be anyone who will abstain from killing the beast in favor of calmly allowing himself to be bitten by it. Indeed there will be very few who, bearing in mind the rights of those others of God's creatures, the domestic animals, to life and liberty, will abstain from yoking them or killing them for food.

And by what other right do we isolate those who are mad or suspected of contagious disease? Precisely because it is based on fact. The penal theory founded on the need for defence is the least subject to contradiction.

At one time punishment, taking on the colouring and origins of the crime, and atavistic in any case, was, and made no effort to hide the fact, either a compensation or a vendetta. The judges were even not ashamed to make themselves into executioners. Crime was considered not merely an evil, but the gravest of all evils, which only death could suffice to punish. If the criminal failed to confess, he was made to do so by means of torture, and time was saved over interrogations. Later, only evidence was required, and what evidence! Sometimes, they even dispensed with this. And not merely did they kill the criminal; they took care to see that he felt death. This could not by any means mitigate the crimes; but cruel though punishments were, there was a certain measure of logic in them. At least the theory did not contradict the practice; they started out from the position that a bad man never reforms, but instead gives birth to sons who are equally bad. They killed the criminal and through death prevented any recurrence of his crime. Better still, there was sincerity in it. They were obeying that instinct, that kind of reflex movement, which impels us to avenge ourselves for one insult by another, but they did not disclaim it. But where is our logic, our sincerity in penal matters? Nowadays we have not lost that primitive instinct. When we judge a criminal, we aim always at proportioning the punishment to the standard of disgust or contempt aroused in us by the crime; but we are scandalised and cry out if anyone admits to this. This is clear when we hear the representatives of the law forgetting abstract theory and demanding clearly and loudly a social vendetta, only to reject it with holy horror when they come to write a book on penal law or when they sit as legislators. And what logic is there ever in the theory for example that is now coming back into vogue which aims to base punishment on the making of amends when we know quite well that the reform is always, or almost always, exceptional, and a return to crime the rule. Prison, if not the cell which is generally economically impractical, not only fails to reform the criminal, but depraves him still further; and is indeed a school of evil!

Oppenheim, after writing that no crime should go without its proportional form of punishment, says that the punishment itself is evil and goes so far as to say "Punishment should only consist of reforming and occupying the criminal." But is there not a clear contradiction here? How can we accept a theory which dishonours the criminal and at the same time aspires to reform him? How can we brand him on the forehead and then tell him to reform himself?

What else are the theories of penal retribution of Herbart, Kant, Altomid, Hegel and De Ercole if not the ancient concepts of vendetta and retaliation in disguise? According to Altomid, the State should inflict as much hurt on the criminal as he has inflicted on his victim. This is the old formula of an eye for an eye and a tooth for a tooth. But the State is not looking ahead; it shuts up the criminal, punishes him and then releases him again, leaving the community in a continuing, and what is worse, an increasing danger, since the criminal in contact with other prisoners becomes still worse.

Certain legislators have said: the criminal must do penance. But the conception of penance is ecclesiastical, depending on an act of free will. Can we use the expression to describe the act of a criminal whose life or liberty are removed by force?

Criminal lawyers like Seiferteld make crime dependent on depraved free will, turning to the ancient theory of perversity. But to admit, as they do, the attenuating circumstances is to contradict oneself straight away and admit of a diminished state of freedom.

The theory of intimidation or example also provides plenty of contradictions. Our ancestors set up whipping posts, tore off noses and ears, quartered, drowned in oil or boiling water, poured molten lead down necks, cut the loins out of the living flesh. But with what results? Only that of producing still more numerous and frightful crimes.

But if the ancients produced all this with so much torture, what shall we obtain now with half measures, now that the publicity has rightfully been taken from torture as though the community were ashamed of it, and that prison, for some people, has become a home from home?

And again, what justice is there in punishing a man, not so much for what he has done as for what others might do?

As for the theory of some of our people who consider punishment as a legitimate act of the social power, whereby just so much restriction on liberty is inflicted as is required for reintegration in the juridical order, I, being unequipped with such sublime juridical abstractions, confess that I am unable to form any clear idea far removed from that of Kant. But if this definition really does lead one to consider punishment as a just evil which is inflicted, for the safety of good order, on any person committing an unjust evil, I should be in complete agreement. This would be the defence theory. Naturally I should find it strange and audacious to attempt to deduce from the spider's web of a definition, however sublime and complete it might be, a whole penal system which would decide for thousands of lives. It would be too much to credit human ingenuity with the construction of such a complete system or to prefer a momentary flash of genius to patient observation of the facts.

GABRIEL TARDE
(1843–1904)

Jean Gabriel Tarde was born in Sarlat, France in 1843 and attended the Jesuit school there. It is said of Tarde—as it was said of Beccaria and Lombroso before him—that, although he profited from a scholastic education, he was sorely chafed by the Jesuitical discipline. Among his studies, Tarde excelled in mathematics and probably would have attended the Ecole Polytechnique but for the fact that he contracted an eye disease which considerably reduced his ability to read. He entered upon what was a somewhat less demanding course of study in law at Toulouse and later in Paris.

After completing his legal studies, Tarde took several judicial posts in the region of his birthplace. Such was the nature of his judicial duties that he had ample time to embark on a career of research and writing in criminology and sociology seldom equaled in his day or even in our own.

In criminology, Tarde's approach is noted for its even-handed emphasis on both social and individual factors in crime causation—though he did altogether reject the biological theories of the Italian school. His criticism directed specifically at Lombroso was reasoned and well-supported by data. It has been said that Tarde's criticism was so effective, in fact, that it seriously dampened Lombroso's popularity in France.

Probably the best known of Tarde's criminological theories is that making use of his "laws of imitation." Basically, these state that persons acquire criminal behavior patterns by learning them from others. At one point, Tarde envisions criminals as a "professional type," having acquired their criminal traits through apprenticeship in a milieu where criminogenic influences predominate.

Tarde was perhaps as close to modern American criminology as any of the major theorists in the history of the discipline. His "laws of imitation" bear a strong resemblance to Sutherland's "differential association theory" as does his analysis of the "professional type" of criminal to Sutherland's "professional thief."

GABRIEL TARDE

Penal Philosophy

THE CRIMINAL

The Criminal Type. What is a criminal?—At the death of the great Lama, the priests of Thibet agree to seek for the newborn into whom his immortal soul has transmigrated. They recognize him by certain characteristics, by true anthropological description, which they firmly believe never deceives. The Egyptian priests proceeded in exactly the same way, in order to pick out the bull Apis among all the bulls in the Valley of the Nile. Thus, there was for them, as there still is for the clergy and the people of Thibet, a divine type; and it is thus that in the eyes of Lombroso a criminal type exists which will allow of recognizing the malefactor from birth. Such, at least, was his first conception; but we know that in being developed it could not help becoming complicated in order to accommodate itself to the facts that contradicted it. At the present time, what is there left of it? Apparently, there is little, but, at the same time, something essential, as we shall see. If it had only served to give us more precise knowledge as to what the criminal is not, without giving a single indication, moreover, as to what he is, it would not have been in vain. But it has done more. It has accumulated curious observations, which will doubtless be useful later on; it has outlined in characteristics which will not perish the psychology of the delinquent, and has paved the way for a sociological explanation of him.

First of all, owing to the partial failure of its attempt, the school of Lombroso seems to us to have absolutely demonstrated that the criminal is not a product of nature; that is to say, that he does not correspond to any natural idea in the Platonic sense, nor in the scientific sense either. Combine by Galton's process ten or a dozen photographs of Chinamen, and you will obtain a generic portrait wherein, with their differences blotted out, their similarities alone will appear in a curious relief, a living abstraction and individual incarnation of the ideal rule, of which the individuals are the oscillating deviations. This picture-type has this particular thing about it, that it embellishes that which it combines and it explains that which it sums up. Carry out the same operation with twenty or thirty other Chinamen; the new synthetic picture will resemble the preceding one still more than the photographs which compose it resemble one another.

One would perceive this by operating separately upon various groups in this album. The number of groups would determine the number of results, which would differ very greatly from one another and would have scarcely any more relation with the elementary portraits which had been violently disintegrated and artificially combined in them. Can one at least hope that in separately photographing groups of malefactors belonging to the same category,—"caroubleurs" (thieves who use false keys), "cambrioleurs" (robbers of apartments), "escarpes" (assassins), swindlers and "stupratori,"—one might be more fortunate? Not at all. Each nation and each race has its swindlers, its thieves, and its assassins, who are bearers of the anthropological characteristics that distinguish it. With any physical type, under certain social conditions, and being given certain cerebral peculiarities that are too profound to reveal themselves in the external anatomy, one can create delinquents of every kind. Thus there are no more *several* criminal types than *one* criminal type in the *Lombrosian* sense of the word; and Marro, when he attempts to substitute the plural here for the singular, is no less conjectural and has no better foundation than his master. One of two things must be so. Either the delinquent is physically, if not physiologically, normal, and in this case he bears the very type of his country, or else he is abnormal, and then he does not belong to any type; and it is his very lack of type that characterizes him. But, to say at the same time that he is an anomaly and that he conforms to a natural model is to contradict oneself. There is another hidden contradiction in looking upon the social life as so essential to man that a human being who is "dishumanized," so to speak, can alone be antisocial, and to assume that nature has taken the pains to make a special creation in order to bring forth this individual who is contrary to nature.

Thus, if there existed a criminal type, this type would be subject to fluctuation and changes which, from century to century and from latitude to latitude, could not fail to render him exceedingly unlike himself. A few skulls, a few brains of assassins, weighed and measured in our time,—this is all very well. But have there been submitted to the same anthropological examination the thousands of thieves hanged yearly upon the gallows of England within the last half century, the people sacrificed at Montfaucon, the corpses swinging in the breeze before the gateways of the feudal castles, upon all the hills, before the entrance of every town of the Middle Ages? The twenty thousand heretics and sorcerers burned in eight years by Torquemada, the Romans condemned to be given to the beasts or to be handed over to the games of the circus, and the Egyptians condemned to labor in the mines or upon the pyramids? All those pirates of Barbary who infested the Mediterranean until the end of the last century, all those highwaymen who devastated France during and after the Hundred Years War,— who will tell us the form of their skulls and their cerebral or corporeal anomalies, if anomalies there were? Who will verify, by referring to them, the exactness of the pretended proper types, we are asked, of the malefactors of every race and of all times?

The Criminal Type is a Professional Type. If the group of malefactors, which is as variegated as it is numerous, as changing as it is persistent, is not united by a single bond that is truly vital; if there exist between them neither that pathological relationship which a similar form of degeneracy or mental alienation would establish, a same group of maladies with which they would be affected, nor that physiological relationship which their common resemblance to supposed ancestors would bear witness to, of what nature, then, is the bond which brings them together and often gives them a special physiognomy more easily perceived than formulated? In our opinion it is a bond which is entirely social, the intimate relation which is to be observed between people carrying on the same trade or trades of a similar character; and this hypothesis is sufficient to account for even the anatomical peculiarities, especially the physiological and psychological peculiarities by which delinquents are distinguished. Let us first deal with the former.

We have told in a previous chapter why every profession, whether it be open to everybody or enclosed in a caste, must in the long run recruit its members from among those individuals best endowed and best fitted to succeed in it, or develop among its members, through heredity, the talents and, consequently, the forms which it prefers. This is so not only with regard to every profession, but with regard to every class and every social category that is more or less clearly defined. For example, a series of the skulls of *distinguished men*—by this is understood the chosen of the liberal professions collectively—is typified, according to Manouvrier, by a face which is relatively small, a fine frontal development, and especially a cubic capacity that is far above the average. When we go into detail in the separate study of artists, learned men, philosophers, or engineers, we shall certainly be led to draw a typical portrait which will have rather strong characteristics drawn from each one of these groups. It is even probable that it might easily be clearer and less doubtful than the famous criminal type.

As a matter of fact, of all careers, the career of a criminal is indeed the one that is least often entered into by a person having freedom to choose, and is the one where, as a consequence of the rapid extinction of vicious families, the hereditary transmission of aptitudes has less time to be carried out. One has been thrust into it from birth; this is the ordinary case. The majority of murderers and notorious thieves began as children who had been abandoned, and the true seminary of crime must be sought for upon each public square or each crossroad of our towns, whether they be small or large, in those flocks of pillaging street urchins who, like bands of sparrows, associate together, at first for marauding, and then for theft, because of a lack of education and food in their homes. Without any natural predisposition on their part, their fate is often decided by the influence of their comrades.

There is not one of even the most precocious of the young monsters of seventeen or eighteen years whose exploits appall the press who has not behind him years of criminal apprenticeship during his entire vagabond and soiled childhood. For the trade of crime, like every other, has its special schools. Also, like every other trade, it has its special idiom, namely, slang. What old and deep-rooted profession has not its own slang, from sailors, masons, and coppersmiths to painters and lawyers,—to the very police agents themselves, who say that they "camoufler" themselves when they mean to "disguise" themselves, and "coton" for a "resemblance," etc.? We can read Maxime du Camp on this subject. Finally, there are special associations, temporary or permanent, epidemic or endemic. As an example of the former, the rising of the peasants in 1358, and in certain respects Jacobinism, which temporarily ravaged France; as an example of the latter, the Camorra and the Maffia, which are traditionally prevalent in Italy. These are great professional syndicates of crime, which have played a far more important historic part than one might suppose. How many times has a warlike band, organized in the very midst of pastoral tribes, been a society of brigands? How many times has this brigandage been the necessary leaven that has served to raise an empire and establish peace through the triumph of the strong?

So, do not reproach me with doing too much honor to crime by placing it among the professions. If the petty criminal industry which languishes in the depths of our towns, like so many little shops where a backward manufacture survives, does nothing but harm, the great criminal industry has had its days of great and fearful utility in the past, under its military and despotic form; and, under its financial form, people pretend that it renders appreciable services. Where would we be if there had never been any fortunate criminals, eager to overcome scruples, rights, prejudices, and customs in order to drive the human race from the pastoral poem to the drama of civilization? And must we not, unfortunately, recognize the fact that from the out and out criminal to the most honest merchant we pass through a series of transitions, that every tradesman who cheats his clients is a thief, that every grocer who adulterates his wine is a poisoner, and that, as a general thing, every man who misrepresents his merchandise is a forger? And I do not mention the great number of industries that exist more or less indirectly through the profits of crime,—low taverns, houses of prostitution, gambling houses, old-clothes shops,—which are just so many places of refuge for the receipt of stolen goods for delinquents. They have many other accomplices. Among the upper classes, how much extortion, how many doubtful bargains, how much traffic in decorations, demand the complicity of people who are rich and reputed to be honest, who profit by them, not always without their knowledge! If the tree of crime, with all its roots and its rootlets, could ever be uprooted from our society, it would leave a giant abyss.

Psychology and the Criminal. Perhaps one is born vicious, but it is quite certain that one becomes a criminal. The psychology of the murderer is, in the last analysis, the psychology of everybody; and in order to go down into his heart it will be sufficient if we analyze our own. One could without any very great difficulty write a treatise upon the art of becoming an assassin. Keep bad company; allow pride, vanity, envy, and hatred to grow in you out of all proportion; close your heart to tender feelings, and only open it to keen sensations; suffer also,—harden yourself from childhood to blows, to intemperateness, to physical torments; grow hardened to evil, and insensible, and you will not be long in becoming devoid of pity; become irascible and vengeful, and you will be very lucky if you do not kill anybody during the course of your life.

Ordinarily, we account for the sudden downfall produced by the first step along the path of vice or crime by saying that a taste for the forbidden fruit or the taste for blood has awakened vicious or precocious instincts. Again, we say that the fault lies with society, which is all too ready to repel the one who falls and to force him to seek shelter in the company of the depraved. But in speaking thus we forget the essential thing, which is the verdict by means of which the internal jury, an echo of outside opinion, cuts off the guilty man from the honest multitude, even before the latter shall have cursed or even blamed him. This imaginary division, with the morbid swelling of self-esteem and the hardening of the heart which follow it, complete his ruin. The more a man feels or thinks himself to be separated from his fellow men because of a fall, or even an assumption of it, because of an infrequent depravity, or even because of an exalted passion, the more dangerous he is. If the prostitutes of our sex are, even more than courtesans, capable of every heinous crime, it is because the feeling of their degradation is especially intense and deep within them.

Again, as long as the fault remains hidden, this ditch which the conscience of the sinner digs between honest people and himself is capable of being filled in. But, when prosecution against him has taken place, and when he has been condemned, the gulf within him becomes singularly widened and deepened by being revealed to the outside world, in the same way that his evil nature, in being revealed to itself because of the crime, had become accentuated and fixed. A woman whose one fault is made public is lost forever. Inevitably, the criminal is the result of his own crime just as much as his crime is his own work; also, inevitably, the criminal is partially the result of criminal justice. Excommunicated in everybody's eyes by this justice, he cuts himself off still more in his own eyes, almost, but in an opposite way, as an artist or poet who, after having been the only one to be aware of his talents, is touched by a ray of fame and at once sees the pedestal which he is erecting for himself grow a thousand cubits.

It is none the less true that, because of the opinion that they hold as to their separation from surrounding society and as to their dissimilarity to it and their independence with regard to it, both the artist and the criminal furnish the proof of their close similarity in spite of everything, and of their forced communication with that common herd which they disdain or curse. In the case of fame, just as in the case of condemnation, the "myself" reflects the opinions of others within its obscure chamber; it cannot help admiring itself even more when it is praised, and disparaging itself even more when it is disparaged; only, this latter attitude of self-esteem being unnatural, the "myself" often compels itself to give back to the honest multitude contempt for contempt, which is only another means of reflecting it while repelling it. Thus the "myself" still remains sufficiently similar to society to retain its responsibility towards it; and, on the other hand, its alienation within itself, which is rather a revelation of a disturbing nature, is far from being sufficiently great to place any obstacle in the way of its responsibility.

The new Italian school repeats to satiety that it is important to study and to punish the reality known as the criminal, and not the entity known as the crime. We see at present with what restrictions we ought to accept this opinion, and that the old school was not without some reason in taking the opposite point of view; or, rather, we perceive the easy and complete reconciliation of the opposite points of view. We also understand why the perpetrator of a great crime, even though it be committed by accident, has from this time on become more dangerous, and should be more severely punished than a petty habitual malefactor. In fact, the more serious the crime that has been carried out, the more honest has the consciousness in which it has burst forth remained up to that time, the deeper and the more terrible is the revolutionary crisis within the "myself" which is the consequence of it. But when from childhood a man has accustomed himself to committing larcenies which are at first insignificant and then become progressively more important, this violent shaking up of his personality has been avoided, and he has never ceased to feel those close ties that he has with surrounding society. To confuse these two categories of guilty men by dealing out to assassins and to recidivists who are misdemeanants the same fate in the colonies is an injustice which is based upon a mistake.

CRIME

Even admitting as certain the anthropological ideas of the new school, it has been possible to observe that they allowed of a sociological interpretation far preferable to the too exclusively biological interpretation which its founders have formulated. In the same way we shall see that, to a lesser degree, it repeats the same mistake in interpreting the statistical statements which are the most serious and perhaps the most lasting foundation of its work. After having, by means of anthropology and mental pathology, sought the typical characteristics of the criminal, it seeks, by means of statistics, to find the natural laws of crime. It accords, as we have said in our statement, a greater part to social causes in the production of crime than in the production of criminal tendencies. In fact, it speaks of the "sociological factors" at the same time as the physical or anthropological factors. Its mistake, in our opinion, is in having placed in the same rank causes so heterogeneous and in having misunderstood the peculiar nature as well as the greater intensity of the first of them. This reproach is not addressed to the socialists of the school, but, among the social causes of crime, the latter refuse to recognize any but economic causes, and their point of view upon this subject is no less imperfect than that of their brother naturalists.

This much having been said, we cannot too highly praise the efforts and the attempts, even though they be sometimes without result, of these distinguished statisticians. Had they done no more than bring to light the regular progress of recidivism in all countries and to bring about the necessary measures to deal with recidivists, they would have a right to our gratitude. Theoretically, they have accomplished more than this. If however they have so far given us nothing more than an outline, if they have not worked for a common object, though they have limited themselves to working out a few isolated problems of social arithmetic, such as the relation of the seasons to the curve of crime, or the relation of the curve of homicides to that of suicides, of the curve of crimes against the person to that of crimes against property, etc.; the relations between certain facts which they have established are valuable acquisitions to science. In this they resemble the psycho-physicians whose contributions to psychology bear upon points which are as yet secondary, but have the advantage of introducing for the first time precision and certainty, "aliquid inconcussum," and are stepping-stones to the future. Only, the psychologist who, upon the limited basis of his own experiments, should hasten to reconstruct at the present time the whole of psychology, would run a very serious risk of being mistaken.

PART PLAYED BY PHYSICAL AND PHYSIOLOGICAL INFLUENCES

When statistics first came into operation, the facts primarily revealed by them seemed completely to overthrow accepted ideas. Then great was the surprise at the fact of the establishment of that annual reproduction of figures which were approximately the same with respect to the same offenses. At first this unvarying contingent was looked upon as being irreconcilable with free will, and, as it was customary to base responsibility upon free will, the conclusion was soon arrived at that the criminal is not responsible for the crime committed by him. No doubt in the beginning the invariableness of the part contributed by the criminal, with which we are concerned, was greatly exaggerated; but the variations which were noticed in it later on also showed themselves to be regular, and subject to periods of very high or very low continuance.

Now in what way is the regularity or merely the continuance of these variations here less capable of being opposed to the assumption of individual liberty than is the exactness of these repetitions? Thus, the objection which was made at the outset continues in full force, and only habit has in the end weakened it. As to the replies which have been made to this objection, they can be classified into two parts, the one of a despairing weakness, the other of a despairing obscurity. The most specious of them consists in saying with Quételet, that free decisions, in so far as they are peculiar and accidental, play the part of the disturbances of an astronomic curve and neutralize one another.

This is an illusory explanation. Let us assume an astronomical curve resulting from the combined effects of disturbances exclusively. This is indeed our very case, as all crimes, all marriages, and all the purchases carried out in a certain situation during one year are considered as emanating from the independent initiative of individuals. It remains to show in what manner these initiatives can neutralize one another, and how, a deduction having been made for their so-called neutralizations, we arrive at a numerical remainder equal to or in conformity with a certain empirical law of increase or decrease. Now, this absolute or relative uniformity would be incomprehensible if we did not admit that wills, looked upon as independent *in law,* make, so to speak, absolutely no use *in fact* of their independence, and that they constantly correspond to a sum which is equal, or regularly increasing and decreasing, of influences of a social, or vital or physical order, in comparison with which the part which can be attributed to their freedom is a negligible quantity.

As to the regular variations, which anthropometry would have no difficulty in disclosing, were it to be applied to hybrid races in process of formation or disappearance, their regularity would also demonstrate the preponderating effect exercised by the hereditary propagation of certain organic modifications. If, to assume what is impossible, all these were but original variations in the living being, if each individual were a species apart, though one were to count a thousand, ten thousand, ten million statures or heart pulsations, one would never arrive at figures which would be approximately reproduced when one began to take these same measurements on other subjects. The law of great numbers would serve no purpose, and again, the more the number of observations was increased, far from becoming less, the greater would become the inconsistency of the figures.

Everything I have just said is applicable, "mutatis mutandis," to moral statistics. If, in the determining by each citizen of each one of the acts of his life, marriage for example, the part played by free initiative, released from all physical, vital, or social suggestion, preponderated or were even appreciable, we would not see the number of marriages, in a given locality and during a stated period of time, recurring every year with a striking monotony, or following a progress no less remarkable. But the concurrence of the three sorts of influences pointed out exercises upon the total number of wills an all-powerful effect, because here more marked, there less marked,—as we see the printing of a same negative result in proofs which are either too pale or too dark, but generally resembling one another,—it is only combated to a very small extent by individual spontaneity.

The three sorts of influences are very clearly to be distinguished in the example which has been chosen by reason of the sensitive test of statistics; for it is quite certain that it is an impulse which is physiological, hereditary, and which varies according to age, as well as an impulse which is physical and varies according to the season, which drives men to marriage. But it is also a social impulse, a carrying away by custom or surrounding example. Were it not for this there would be nothing but free unions, and not any official marriages, civil any more than religious. Thus the regularity of the statistics of marriage only proves one thing, which is, that the force of *imitation-custom* is constant in this respect, or else regularly increasing or decreasing because of its coming into contact with *imitation-fashions* whose propagation is favorable or unfavorable to it, and that it is far more intense than the force of individual initiative, independent of tradition or opinion. *The quantitative superiority of voluntary energies subjected to Imitation over voluntary energies employed along the lines of Innovation*; here indeed, we have the sum total of what is expressed by the regular figures of social statistics.

PREPONDERANCE OF SOCIAL CAUSES

The Tendency Towards Imitation. Before anything else, we ought summarily to define and analyze the powerful, generally unconscious, always partly mysterious, action by means of which we account for all the phenomena of society, namely imitation. In order to judge of its inherent power, we must first of all observe its manifestations among idiots. In them the imitative inclination is no stronger than in ourselves, but it acts without encountering the obstacle which is met with in our ideas, our moral habits, and our wishes. Now, a case is cited of an idiot who "after having taken part in the slaughtering of a pig took a knife and attacked a man." Others carry out the imitative tendency in setting fire to buildings.

All the important acts of social life are carried out under the domination of example. One procreates or one does not procreate, because of imitation; the statistics of the birth rate have shown us this. One kills or one does not kill, because of imitation; would we today conceive of the idea of fighting a duel or of declaring war, if we did not know that these things had always been done in the country which we inhabit? One kills oneself or one does not kill oneself, because of imitation; it is a recognized fact that suicide is an imitative phenomenon to the very highest degree; at any rate it is impossible to refuse to give this character to those "suicides in large numbers of conquered peoples escaping by means of death the shame of defeat and the yoke of the stranger, like that of the Sidonians who were defeated by Artaxerxes Orchus, of the Tyrians defeated by Alexander, of the Sagontines defeated by Scipio, of the Achaeans defeated by Metellus, etc."

After this how can we doubt but that one steals or does not steal, one assassinates or does not assassinate, because of imitation? But it is especially in the great tumultuous assemblages of our cities that this characteristic force of the social world ought to be studied. The great scenes of our revolutions cause it to break out, just as great storms are a manifestation of the presence of the electricity in the atmosphere, while it remains unperceived though none the less a reality in the intervals between them. A *mob* is a strange phenomenon. It is a gathering of heterogeneous elements, unknown to one another; but as soon as a spark of passion, having flashed out from one of these elements, electrifies this confused mass, there takes place a sort of sudden organization, a spontaneous generation. This incoherence becomes cohesion, this noise becomes a voice, and these thousands of men crowded together soon form but a single animal, a wild beast without a name, which marches to its goal with an irresistible finality. The majority of these men had assembled out of pure curiosity, but the fever of some of them soon reached the minds of all, and in all of them there arose a delirium. The very man who had come running to oppose the murder of an innocent person is one of the first to be seized with the homicidal contagion, and moreover, it does not occur to him to be astonished at this.

The Laws of Imitation. After these few words as to the force and the forms of imitation, we must set forth its general laws, which must be applied to crime as well as to every other aspect of societies. But the limits of this work will only allow us a brief indication of the subject. We already know that the example of any man, almost like the attraction of a body, radiates around himself, but with an intensity which becomes weaker as the distance of the men touched by his ray increases. "Distance" should not here be understood merely in the geometrical sense, but especially in the psychological sense of the word; the increase in the relations established by correspondence or by printing, of the intellectual communications of all kinds between fellow-citizens scattered over a vast territory, has the effect of diminishing in this sense the distance between them. Thus it may happen, let us repeat, that the honest example of an entire surrounding but distant society may be neutralized in the heart of a young vagabond by the influence of a few companions. From the economic, philological, religious, and political point of view, it is the same.

It is especially in fostering the spread of example that a social hierarchy is useful; an aristocracy is a fountain reservoir necessary for the fall of imitation in successive cascades, successively enlarged. If industry on a large scale has become a possibility in our day, if the diffusion of needs, of tastes, of identical ideas in the hearts of immense masses of people has opened up the vast outlets which it needs, is it not to the old inequalities that we are indebted for this existing equality?

But let us beware of thinking that this movement is going to cease; in democratic times the work of the nobility is carried on, and on a larger scale, by capitals. The latter in many ways resemble the former. The nobility, in their days of splendor, shine by reason of wit, luxury, generosity, courage, gallantry, and a spirit of enterprise; they purchase these brilliant gifts by furnishing a larger contingent to madness, crime, suicide, the duel, illegitimate births, to vices and maladies of every sort. Capitals are no less luxurious, no less ruinous, no less gay and full of innovation. They show the same egoism and the same insolence; they have a profound contempt for the provinces in return for the profound admiration which they themselves inspire in the former, and treat them in precisely the same manner as the gentlemen of former days used to treat the common people, who were only too happy to pay their debts and for their extravagances; they also show a lower birth rate and a higher death rate; and, owing to the cankers which gnaw them, to tuberculosis, syphilis, alcoholism, pauperism, and prostitution, they would inevitably perish if, like every living aristocracy, they were not renewed very quickly by the influx of new elements. They maintain themselves by means of immigration as did the Roman patriarchate by means of adoption. Thus the moralist of today, in order that he may predict what the morality of tomorrow will be, should keep his eye on the examples furnished by great cities, just as the moralist of yesterday was right in being concerned with what took place in the midst of courts, salons, and castles.

While crime formerly spread, like every industrial product, like every good or bad idea, from the nobility to the people, and while the nobility, in those remote times, drew to itself the audacious and criminal elements of the people, today we can see crime spreading from the great cities to the country, from the capitals to the provinces, and these capitals and great cities having an irresistible attraction for the outcasts and scoundrels of the country, or the provinces, who hasten to them to become civilized after their own manner, a new kind of ennobling. For the time being this latter fact is a fortunate one for the provinces, which are being purified by means of this emigration and passing through an era of comparative security. Never, perhaps, in rural regions has there been less fear of assassination and even of robbery with violence than at the present time. But unfortunately the attraction of the great cities for criminals is closely connected with the influence exercised by them over the remainder of the nation, with the fascinating power their example has in all matters. As a consequence it is to be feared that the benefits derived from this betterment of conditions in the provinces is but temporary. The capitals send to the provinces not only their political and literary likes and dislikes, their style of wit or folly, the cut of their clothes, the shape of their hats and their accent, but they also send their crimes and their misdemeanors.

Each variety of murder or theft invented by evil genius is born or takes root in Paris, Marseilles, Lyons, etc., before becoming widespread throughout France. The series of corpses cut to pieces began in 1876 with the Billoir case and was for a long time confined to Paris, Toulouse, and Marseilles; but it was carried on in the Departments of Nièvre, Loir-et-Cher, and Eure-et-Loir. The feminine idea of throwing vitriol in the face of a lover is entirely Parisian; it was the widow Gras who, in 1875, had the honor of inventing this, or rather of re-inventing it. But I know of villages where this seed has borne fruit, and the peasant women themselves now try their hand at the handling of vitriol. In 1881, a young actress, Clotilde J——, threw vitriol over her lover, at Nice. "When she was asked at what time she first thought of avenging herself, 'since the day,' she replied, 'when I read *in a Paris newspaper* an article dealing with the revenge of women.' "

With regard to thefts the same thing applies. There is not a single means of swindling employed at village fairs which did not first see the light of day upon a sidewalk of Paris. "There were," says Corre (in "Crime et suicide"), "following the Pranzini and Prado cases, a few attempts at imitating them on a small scale carried out upon prostitutes. But what more striking example of suggesto-imitative assault could there be than the series of mutilations of women, begun in the month of September 1888 *in London,* in the Whitechapel district! Never perhaps has the pernicious influence of *general news* been more apparent. The newspapers were filled with the exploits of Jack the Ripper, and, in less than a year, as many as eight absolutely identical crimes were committed in various crowded streets of the great city. This is not all; there followed a repetition of these same deeds outside of the capital and very soon there was even a spreading of them abroad. At Southampton attempt to mutilate a child; at Bradford horrible mutilation of another child; at Hamburg murder accompanied by disemboweling of a little girl; in the United States disemboweling of four negroes [Birmingham], disemboweling and mutilation of a colored woman [Milville]; in Honduras disemboweling . . . etc. The Gouffe case had its almost immediate counterpart in Copenhagen. . . . Infectious epidemics spread with the air or the wind; epidemics of crime follow the line of the telegraph."

We shall see that the influence exercised by the example of the great cities over criminality is not only direct, as we have just pointed out, but at the same time and more especially indirect, like that of the old nobility, through the spread and the attraction of their pleasures, their luxuries, and their vices, a forerunner of and a preparation for the contagion of their offenses. They attract the country people because the latter began by imitating them in everything. Thus the progress of this imitation may be measured by the progress of rural emigration, which is almost entirely directed towards Paris or the other great centres. An exodus within and without which is ever increasing, because the proportion of the rural population as compared with the total population is constantly decreasing, and, in less than twenty-five years, has been lowered from three-quarters to two-thirds.

This problem, which has been so much discussed, of the relations which exist between the progress of civilization and the movement or the change in criminality, will have to be stated before it can be solved. We will state it in another way. Criminality always being, in its characteristic form and its realization in fact, a phenomenon of imitative propagation, the question is, whether the many other phenomena of imitative propagation, which taken all together are called civilization—academic diffusion of knowledge, domestic or ecclesiastical diffusion of beliefs and rites, diffusion of political ideas by the newspapers, diffusion of the requirements of consumption through contact with comrades, diffusion of industrial or artistic aptitudes and talents, by the life of the studio, the office, the trade, etc.—foster or impede the progress of the propagation of crime. Or rather, the aim is to discover, if that were possible, which among these various spreadings of example which are called instruction, religion, politics, commerce, industry, are the ones that foster, and which the ones that impede, the expansion of crime.

The manner in which we state the question already shows that in our opinion crime is a peculiar social fact, but after all a social fact like any other. It is an off-shoot of the national tree, but a branch nourished by the common sap and subject to the laws which are common to all. We have seen that, taken by itself, it grows in conformity with the rule of imitation from *above* to *below,* just as do all the other fruitful and useful branches of the same trunk. We might have added that, again like them, it becomes changed or develops through the intermittent insertion of new buds or new grafts of *imitation-fashions* which come to replenish and nourish, sometimes to drive back, a stock of *imitation-customs,* but they themselves have a tendency to take root, to swell the legacy of custom and tradition. Every industry feeds itself in this manner by means of an afflux of improvements, innovations today, traditions tomorrow. Every science, every art, every language, every religion, obeys this law of the passing from custom to fashion and the return from fashion to custom, but custom which has expanded. For with each step in advance taken by it the territorial domain of imitation becomes larger, the field of social assimilation and of human fraternity expands, and it is not, as we know, the least salutary effect of imitative cause from the point of view of morality.

It is useless to insist any further. We can draw the conclusion that every social matter, that is to say, all individual initiative, every special method of thought, feeling, or action, put in circulation by a man, has a tendency to be spread through fashion, among primitive peoples as well as among those who are civilized, and after having become widespread, to take root in the form of a custom, among civilized peoples as well as among primitive ones.

The thing which concerns us is to observe that it is not merely language, dogma, industrial and artistic instruments and talents, but moral or immoral feelings, moral or immoral habits as well, which have a tendency to become general and to become fixed in this manner.

A Summing Up of the Chapter. To sum up this entire chapter, we have every right, it seems to me, to conclude that criminality without any doubt, like every other branch of social activity, implies physiological and even physical conditions, but that, like industry especially, it is to be accounted for better than in any other way, by the general laws of imitation, in its local color as in its special force at each period of time, in its geographical distribution as in its historical transformations, in the varying proportion of its various motives or the unstable hierarchy of its varying degrees as in the succession of its changing methods. We have mentioned the importance in our opinion attaching to this demonstration, from the point of view of penal responsibility, from which it results that the offense is an act emanating not merely from the living being, but from the personal individual, such as society alone can make him and cause him to increase in number in its image; from the person more identical with himself, up to a certain point at least, as he is more similar to others; the more willing and conscious as he is more readily impressed by example, just as the better it breathes, the stronger the lung is. It has been said that our body is a small quantity of condensed air, living in the air. Can it not be said that our soul is a small quantity of society incarnate, living in society? Born from society, it lives by means of society; and if the analogies which I have perhaps at some length enumerated are correct, there is no reason why its criminal responsibility should be misunderstood any more than its civil responsibility, which latter is undisputed and assuredly incapable of being disputed.

Moreover, let us clearly understand each other on this important point. I will not deny that, to a greater or lesser extent, the physical or physiological provocations to commit an offense have acted as the determining cause of the will; but their action, being only partial, does not prevent the delinquent from being responsible. On the contrary, they compete with one another, on their part, to demonstrate that he is responsible. No doubt, if they acted by themselves upon the individual, he would not be socially responsible, because this would reveal in him a being absolutely alien to the society of other men; but he might continue to be responsible individually. By this I mean that the condition of social similarity, required by our theory of responsibility, would not really be fulfilled, but that the condition of individual identity, which is above all requisite, might be realized, in spite of the inevitable necessity of external influences.

Without doubt one can see, to a certain extent, in the criminal calendar, and in general, in all statistical tables where a connection is shown between exciting causes of a physical or vital nature and a recurrence of certain crimes, a *sociological* confirmation of the physio-psychological hypothesis as to the similarity of the will to reflex action. The will, according to this theory, only differs from reflex action in the number of the psychic elements, of the memories interposed between the initial exciting cause and the final reaction, which is called voluntary when one has lost consciousness of the complex tie which exists between these two terms. Thus statistics would give us back this lost consciousness, or rather, it would enable us to acquire this consciousness which we have never had by causing us to put our finger on our secret springs.

Now, this much having been admitted and to a certain extent proved, it is quite certain that responsibility based upon free will falls to the ground. But based upon identity, upon individual *character*, it survives, on condition that social similarity be not lacking. For the exciting cause which has been received has only acted because it has been found to be in accord with the demands of the character; this conformity is one of the necessary intermediaries between the first and the last term of the series. Besides, the true nature of reflex action, even the most simple and of the lowest form, would be misinterpreted if there were seen in it merely a phenomenon of causality without any finality. This elementary reflex, the reflex of organization, to use Richet's term, is the employment of the exciting cause with a view to realizing the ends of the species, of the physical organism. When will is present, "acquired reflex," the reaction is the employment of the exciting cause with a view to the attainment of the individual ends of the person. Let us not forget this mystery of the person; especially let us guard against denying it. To affirm the existence of the unknown, is not this often the only means of turning our lack of knowledge to account? However this may be, should the reflex be greater, the voluntary act would still be ours. But besides this it belongs to society, and, as such, makes us accountable to society, when the exciting causes which have brought it about are partly or mostly social ones.

I would not wish to leave the subject without giving warning that the analogies herein developed as existing between crime and the other social phenomena, especially industry, must not make us forget the differences which exist between them. Crime is a social phenomenon like any other, but a phenomenon which is at the same time anti-social, just as a cancer participates in the life of an organism, but working to bring about its death. And, in fact, if Mitschlerlich was able to say that "life is a corruption," a bitter saying justified to a certain extent by the new school of chemists, according to whom the "chemical diminution of putrefaction and those of the intra-organic combustions offer the greatest analogy," we have a right to say also, as a consequence, that corruption is a part of life, but of the life which kills. Crime is an industry, but a negative one, which accounts for its extreme age; as soon as the first product was manufactured by a laborious tribe, there must have been formed a band of plunderers. A brother and a contemporary of the industry which it fosters, crime does not originally seem to have been any more a disgrace than industry itself. They have developed along the same lines, by both passing from the unilateral form to the bilateral form.

In the beginning, industry was the result of services which were not paid for, given for nothing to the chief by his subjects, to the master by his slaves; by becoming mutual, it has become commerce, an exchange of services. Crime, in becoming mutual, has become warfare, an exchange of injuries. Just as barter and sale is the bilateral form of the gift, so is the duel the bilateral form of homicide, and war the bilateral form not only of homicide, but of plunder, theft, and arson; it is the highest and the most absolute possible expression of crime which has become a mutual affair. The unfortunate part of it is that, although this complex form of crime has made its appearance, simple crime, crime properly so called, has not disappeared. But the same thing is true with regard to simple industry, a partisan of slavery, which does not give way without resistance to free and salaried industry, and in certain countries succeeds in prolonging itself indefinitely alongside of the latter. It is none the less true that free industry is the born enemy of slavery, and that militarism is the born enemy of brigandage. Spencer, as we saw above, was right when he saw in military development the source of penal repression.

This is so for the very reason that war is a result of crime, the soldier a result of the brigand, as the workman is a result of the slave. This derivation is not a doubtful one. The further back we go into the past, the more does the boundary between the army and the plundering band become effaced. In the sixteenth century even, in the civilized States of Europe, there was no hesitation in looking upon brigandage as entitling a man to military advancement. The Spanish army, the best disciplined of all those of that time "found included in its ranks," Forneron tells us, "assassins or brigands who had given themselves up. Sometimes the brigands who were carrying on their trade in the Catalonian mountains allowed themselves, at a time when their trade seemed to be most dangerous, to be formed into companies under the command of one of their leaders, who received a captain's commission, and to be incorporated as a unit into some previously existing regiment. Some useful crime would obtain for a man the rank of an officer."

Until the seventeenth century, even in France, the royal garrisons of towns "were looked upon as a veritable scourge and, whereas now towns ask for the privilege of having a barracks, they used formerly to endeavor to avert this danger; this privilege was appreciated only by those upon whom it was not conferred. The bands of Germans, Italians and Swiss who were in the pay of France conducted themselves during the religious wars and the Fronde as though in a conquered country. The French companies did not behave any better. They all held their prisoners for ransom and plundered defenseless villages." Everywhere armies, even the regular ones, have begun by inspiring as great a dread in their fellow-countrymen as in the enemy.

It is really a surprising thing to find developing side by side during the progress of history, with an increasing breadth and power, on the one hand this exchange of property, this competition between different kinds of produce, which is commerce, and on the other hand, this exchange of injuries, this impact of destructive agencies, which is warfare!

The enormous difference between the simple and the complex, the unilateral and the bilateral, established in this manner between crime and warfare ought not, moreover, to astonish us; this method is a customary one in social logic. Between slavery and the condition of wage earners, between gift and sale, between the command and the contract, between the subjection of woman to man as a result of primitive marriage and their mutual fettering as a result of modern marriage, between homage, which is politeness not reciprocated, and politeness, which is mutual homage, etc., there is no lesser abyss than between murder and combat. It is certain that crime, at the present time at least, serves no useful purpose, and is injurious to everything, whereas war has a very serious reason for existing, one which is inherent in the very heart of society; and in spite of Spencer's error on this subject, the military development of a people is far more often in direct ratio than in inverse ratio to their industrial development. Can it be deduced from this that, before the first wars, murder and theft were in some way of use? Yes, if it be true that the simple is the means of the complex. Was it not necessary to pass through slavery before arriving at the mutual help accorded one another by workers, through the prostrations of subjects of olden times before their king or their lord, before arriving at our bowing in the street? Was it not necessary to go through the system of command and obedience, of the domestic, political, and religious autocracy, before attaining the system of contract, mutual command, and mutual obedience? Without aggressions, without spontaneous rapine, in the early stages of history, would there ever have been later on conquests and great States, an essential condition of every high, peaceful, and honest civilization? The truth of the matter is that crime has become an evil without anything to compensate for it since it has advantageously been replaced by militarism and warfare. An army is a gigantic means of carrying out, by massacre and pillage on a vast scale, the collective designs of hatred, vengeance, or envy, which one nation stirs up against another. Condemned under their individual form, these odious passions, cruelty and greed, seem to be praiseworthy under their collective form. Why? First of all, because they quell many little internal conflicts though they bring about an external one; also, because they lead to a warlike solution of this very difficulty, and to the increase in territory as a result of the peace which is bound to follow. The effect of militarism is to exhaust the criminal passions scattered through every nation, to purify them in concentrating them, and to justify them by making them serve to destroy one another, under the superior form which they thus assume. After all is said and done, war enlarges the sphere of peace, as crime formerly used to enlarge the sphere of honesty. This is the irony of history.

But, in truth, if this is so, I cannot resist indulging in one reflection. In a time like the present, when militarism has so greatly overflowed, is it not doubly distressing to have also to state the proofs of the overflow of crime? It seems as though, if our criminality began to decrease, as it should do, this would not be too great a detriment to our armaments and our military contingents which are every day increasing.

ENRICO FERRI
(1856–1929)

Ferri was born in Mantua, the son of a shopkeeper. Though an undistinguished student early in life, later on, at the University of Bologna, he seemed to find his métier. He prepared his thesis on the subject of free will, proposing for the first time something he was to argue for throughout his career as a criminologist, namely the substitution of a concept of "social responsibility" for what he considered the outmoded dogma of legal or moral responsibility.

Ferri sent a copy of his thesis to Lombroso who commented on it with approval, and—after spending a year in France using the vast store of criminal statistics gathered in that country—he joined Lombroso for a year of study at the University of Turin. The year of statistical analysis in Paris together with the year of study with Lombroso combined to set Ferri in the positivist mold which was characteristic of his methodology from then on.

He took an appointment as Professor of Criminal Law at Bologna for three years and then in 1882 accepted an appointment for four years at Sienna. It was shortly thereafter that Ferri began his political career. He was elected a Deputy to Parliament from the state of Mantua. Though not elected as a socialist, his position became more and more clearly Marxist. It was for this reason, and for having joined the Socialist Labor Party in 1893, that Ferri lost the professorial chair he had inherited in 1890 from Francesco Carrara at Pisa. He then embarked on a series of public lectures in an effort at popular political education. Throughout this period, however, he never neglected his scholarly tasks. He founded the journal La Scoula Positiva in 1892 and the School for Applied Criminal Law and Procedure in Rome in 1912. He also continued to write and revise his works in criminal law and criminology, lent his considerable services to various congresses and commissions, and offered numerous lectures at universities.

Ferri's prime interests in criminology form a logical and interrelated order. Early in his career, in his university thesis in fact, he suggested that a system of social responsibility be substituted for legal responsibility. This meant that every individual was responsible to the society of which he was a member for the harm he caused irrespective of his *intent or state of mind. However, if the classical definition of responsibility was to give way, so also was the classical scheme of punishment. In place of this there was to be a system of "penal substitutes," processes involving the offender where he either indemnified the society which he had harmed or underwent a program of treatment whereby he would be rendered less likely to be a danger to society in the future.*

In order to carry out such a program, it would be necessary to define the sort of danger the offender represented; and, since Ferri believed that strict individualization was not possible, he suggested a typology of offenders. However, in order to insure empirical validity in such a classification, it would be necessary to adopt a methodology in regard to the analysis of criminal behavior, at once positivistic and at the same time eclectic. It is at this point that Ferri becomes of prime interest for analytical criminology in taking the positivistic approach of Lombroso and applying it to a wide variety of data far beyond its original anthropological limits, and in forming from the resulting data a workable classification of offenders.

ENRICO FERRI

Criminal Sociology*

CRIMINAL SOCIOLOGY

The Programme. [T]he positive criminal school does not consist, as it seems convenient for many of its critics to feign to believe, only in the anthropological study of the criminal; it constitutes a complete renovation,—a radical change of scientific method in the study of criminal social pathology and in the study of what is most effectual among the social and juridical remedies that social pathology presents. The science of crimes and punishments was formerly a doctrinal exposition of the syllogisms brought forth by the sole force of logical phantasy. Our school has made of it a science of positive observation, which, based on anthropology, psychology, and criminal statistics as well as on criminal law and studies relative to imprisonment, becomes the synthetic science to which I myself gave the name "Criminal Sociology." Who would have said that the observations of Laplace on the nebular theory, the voyages of exploration in savage lands, the first studies of Camper, White, and Blumenbach of measurements of the human skull and skeleton, the researches of Darwin on the variations obtained in breeding cattle, or the observations of Haeckel in embryology—might some day be of interest to criminal law? With the present division of scientific labor, it becomes difficult to foresee the possible connection between branches of science so diverse and so far removed from one another. And yet it was these astronomical observations, these recitals of travel which show in the savages of to-day the infancy of primitive

---

* From *Criminal Sociology* by Enrico Ferri. Copyright 1917, 1945 by Little, Brown and Company. Reprinted by special permission of Little, Brown and Company.

humanity and also these zoölogical and anthropological investigations, that gave birth to the first idea, yielding repeated proofs of the universal law of evolution which has dominated and renewed the whole scientific world, not excepting the moral and social sciences, among which definitely figures criminal law. And it is with these discoveries, intimately concerning man, that the criminologist of to-day must occupy himself, in order to seek from the experimental sciences, a positive base for his juridical and social conceptions, unless he consents to resign himself to that mere exercise of rhetoric to which daily practice in the criminal courts gives the lie.

The juridical valuation of criminal acts strictly concerns the criminologist. There are two main reasons why he can no longer put off considering it. The first is to prevent laymen drawing extravagant and erroneous conclusions from the facts which belie the old theories; the second, that while the other juridical sciences are concerned with social relations (abstracting individual particularities which do not directly change their value)—the doctrine of crimes and punishment, unlike them, has man, as he really lives and acts in the social medium, as its immediate object. It is clear that the classical criminologists would oppose this new scientific movement, were it only through the force of inertia. Accustomed as they are to build abstract theories with the aid of pure logic and without other tools than paper, pen, ink, and the volumes of their predecessors, it is natural that they should regret finding themselves forced, if not to make personal researches, at least to procure some positive knowledge of anthropology, psychology, and statistics. But the historical reasons for modern scientific thought, as we have indicated them above, render an increasing complexity in the science of crimes and punishments inevitable, arising from the law that things must develop in becoming more and more complex which is so in the physical as well as in the intellectual and moral order. Now in recapitulating the most serious and most flagrant divergences between the new results of the positive sciences (which study man as a physio-psychic organism, born and living in the midst of a fixed physical and social medium) and the metaphysical doctrines on crime punishment and penal justice of the past, I think I can reduce them to the following points.

Among the fundamental bases of criminal and penal law as heretofore understood are these three postulates:

1. The criminal has the same ideas, the same sentiments as any other man.

2. The principal effect of punishment is to arrest the excess and the increase of crime.

3. Man is endowed with free will or moral liberty; and for that reason, is morally guilty and legally responsible for his crimes.

On the other hand, one has only to go out of the scholastic circle of juridical studies and "a priori" affirmations, to find in opposition to the preceding assertions, these conclusions of the experimental sciences:

1. Anthropology shows by facts that the delinquent is not a normal man; that on the contrary he represents a special class, a variation of the human race through organic and psychical abnormalities, either hereditary or acquired.

2. Statistics prove that the appearance, increase, decrease, or disappearance of crime depends upon other reasons than the punishments prescribed by the codes and applied by the courts.

3. Positive psychology has demonstrated that the pretended free will is a purely subjective illusion.

At first glance it would seem that the new conclusions founded on facts could be nothing less than the funeral oration of penal law. Indeed, this might have been dreaded, did we not believe that every social phenomenon and every institution, far from being the result of human caprice or arbitrary establishment is, on the contrary, a necessary consequence of conditions natural to the existence of humanity and that for this reason as long as these conditions be not essentially changed—which until now has not happened—the foundation itself of these institutions must subsist whatever change may take place in the manner of sustaining, studying, and regulating them in conformity with new conditions, founded on facts. The very purpose of this work is to prove that penal law, whether as a function exercised by society in self-defense, or as a collection of scientific principles intended to regulate this function, always has its reasons for existence. But it will at the same time point out the thorough renovation which is being produced in the spirit and in the practical applications of penal law. And this renovation finds its synthetic expression in the following declaration: We should henceforth devote ourselves not to doctrinal criminal law but to positive criminal sociology in the sense and with the results that I shall develop in the following chapters.

Biological Abnormalities as Basis of Origin and Nature of Delinquency. Each of [the] biological explanations of criminality is true in part. I say in part because each of them is verified more or less completely by facts, in such or such a variety of each category. But none of these hypotheses is sufficient nor complete; first, because they are not sufficient to explain the natural genesis of crime in all the categories of delinquents; in the second place, even when they agree with the characteristics of a given criminal type, they still fall short of giving the precise and fundamental reason why in some individuals a given condition of biological abnormality presages crime while in others only insanity, suicide, or simply an organic and psychic inferiority. Why is it, that of a hundred insane subjects, either neuropathic, neurasthenic, epileptic, degenerate, defective in the nutrition of the nervous system or of the inhibital centers, or who show general anomalies, there are only twenty, thirty, or fifty who commit crimes while the others do not? In some of the cases a satisfactory reply may be given that the others may be influenced by a favorable physical and social environment, which instead of turning the balance to the side of their biological anomaly, restricts it and prevents them from passing to excesses rising to the grade of crime. Even this does not fully explain; for there are degenerates and madmen, living in about the same family and social environment, some of whom become delinquents while others do not, and some become sanguinary and violent, while others, with an organic repugnance to homicide, commit thefts or frauds, and vice versa. The varying differences of exterior circumstances, which are inevitable for each moment of life and for each individual, do not explain this enormous difference in the final result. Of two idiots similarly treated in their family and subject to the same influences, one responds to pleasantries by murder and the other not. Of two degenerates or two insane persons who are refused in marriage, one kills the young woman and the other kills himself at her feet. Of two or more degenerates or neurasthenics, as the result of poverty, one becomes merely an inoffensive vagabond who does nothing worse than beg, while another devotes himself to theft and even to violent robbery accompanied by murder. There is no explanation for the differences, and a thousand other illustrations could be cited. It is useless to say, as does Manouvrier, that two individuals, even living in the same family, never find themselves in exactly identical conditions of environment, because, although true in an abstract and metaphysical way, yet in reality the little differences of circumstances and environment, as between brothers living in the same family, are not a cause proportionate to the enormous difference of results, where one, for instance, remains honest and the other becomes a murderer, or where one of them to escape poverty prefers suicide to murder. The fact is that the biological factor of criminality, the criminal temperament, consists in something specific that has not yet been determined, but without which there is no explanation of such diverse results, out of all proportion to the exterior circumstances in which are often found individuals of every social class tainted with some stigmata of organic or physical anomaly. I become more fixed in this conclusion when I think of the criminal type which serves to distinguish delinquents not only from normal individuals but also from the insane, the degenerates, epileptics, and non-delinquent neurasthenics.

A study of the inmates of an ordinary insane asylum, such as I made at Pesaro and at Bologna, is enough to at once establish this fact. A great majority of these unfortunates do not show the criminal type (especially in the physiognomy), while on the contrary, in a small number of insane who have committed crime, the criminal type is frequent. The well-defined type of the murderer, such as I distinguished it in one young soldier out of seven hundred, I have met with in only three or four insane persons in the asylum of Pesaro; and in the same way that the soldier told me he had been convicted of homicide in his infancy, these insane persons proved to have been tried for murder. I can distinguish the homicide type among a hundred persons affected with general degeneracy or epilepsy or neurasthenia. And inversely, in the asylum for the criminal insane at Montelupo, I found a great number of criminal types always cleanly divisible into murderers and nonviolent thieves, for the simple reason that there are there confined, not ordinary insane and degenerates, but delinquent madmen and degenerates. This does not contradict the fact that there are on the other hand some delinquent degenerates who do not show the criminal type and who have observable symptoms of only serious degeneracy. This is because a very serious degeneracy may efface the specific marks of criminality in its external manifestations.

This amounts to saying that criminality, especially when congenital (but in part when occasional), is a really specific form of biological anomaly, which in the field of race and temperament, is distinguishable from every other form of anomaly, pathology, or degeneracy, and leads precisely to active crime, when favored by given physical and social conditions that offer to the predisposition of the individual the occasion and the means. Hence, not as explaining the essence or nature of criminality but simply because it is necessary to give expression to my thought, I believe that the most accurate and most positive conception from the biological standpoint, is that of a "criminal neurosis," distinct in itself from any pathological, atavic, degenerative, or other form whatsoever: a criminal neurosis that one might again term, with Virgilio, a form of "psychic teratology," with which are certainly associated in a given delinquent in a more or less predominant way, some characteristics of atavism, retarded development, neurasthenia, or degeneracy, but which of itself constitutes the specific factor whereby a particular individual, with certain biological characteristics and exposed to certain influences of physical and social environment commits a given crime. If I wished to attempt one further step in advance I might repeat what I have said elsewhere; namely, that the condition of physio-psychic anomaly (through atavism, pathology, and degeneracy), while affecting the whole nervous system and organism of the individual, may preferentially attack the intelligence, the affections, or the will, and that in the first case we would have insanity, in the second, crime, and in the third, suicide, it being conceded that insanity is the shipwreck of the intelligence, that crime is the lack or loss of the moral or social sense, and that suicide is the bankruptcy of the will in the struggle for existence. Be that as it may, the substance of my thought returns to the point where it attributes to criminality of whatever form and category, a complex origin and nature, both biological (in the specific sense indicated above), as well as physical and social. As for the biological factor considered separately, crime is explicable only by the special and characteristic condition, called for want of a more exact term "criminal neurosis," so also no crime, no matter how insignificant, can be positively explained, unless it be considered as the resultant not only of the biological factor but also of the physical and social factors. Certainly the predominance of a given order of factors determines the distinctions in the mass of delinquents, in accordance with a classification which we shall see later. But it is also certain that every delinquent and every crime of any category, is the simultaneous product of the concurrence of these three natural orders. This synthetic explanation of the origin and nature of crime has never been directly attacked either by the metaphysical critics or by the positivists of the new school. They thus implicitly admit that it is true and complete: after some criticism of detail on particular points of the natural genesis of crime, they even gave the impression that they were entitled to the credit for this proposition of the concurrence of the different criminal factors which we have asserted from the beginning.

Basis of Origin and Nature of Crime Complex. Let us repeat once more that in our opinion crime is not an exclusively biological phenomenon nor the exclusive product of the physical and social environment, but that every crime, trivial or grave, is always the resultant in every anthropological category of delinquents and in every individual of the category, both of a special, permanent or transitory, congenital or acquired abnormality of the organic or psychic constitution, and of external physical and social circumstances which concur in a given time and place in determining the action of a given man. Of this I have furnished a demonstration and an example in my own positivistic researches on the murderer. Let us finally repeat, nevertheless, that in every delinquent whomsoever and in every crime whatever committed by him, the determinating predominance varies, whether it be the predominance of one of the three orders of criminal causation, or the predominance, in either of these orders, of one of the particular causes. Murders committed by the insane are largely the effect of the psychopathological condition of the individual; but this would not be sufficient to cause murder, if it were not, in the first place, of a nature to give the impulsion toward this crime (for otherwise the madman, instead of killing another, would kill himself or would fall into simple delirium) and unless, in the second place, the physical and social conditions concurred here also, although in a lesser degree.

Ten degrees less of heat, or a few millimeters more of barometric pressure on the particular day might perhaps have prevented the murder. So also, if the victim had not met the madman or if the latter had been better guarded and cared for, the homicide would not have occurred. The same may be said of murder committed through congenital tendencies to savagery, without any clinical form of mental alienation. At the opposite extreme, homicide caused by a political ideal (and not by party revenge) is largely the effect of the political and social conditions of environment. But its complete explanation is only to be had by considering also the physical conditions, the action of which, in this case, will not be obvious and might easily escape notice, although none the less real. A hot wind, an excessive and stifling heat, may diminish the nervous energy of the individual and lead him to postpone his act until to-morrow and to-morrow it may be no longer possible. The victim may have gone away or have been warned. A mild temperature and stimulating air may, on the contrary, heighten the resolution and concur in the execution of a political murder. Nor may one at all disregard the biological factor in this case. It is true that one who commits homicide in obedience to a political ideal has nothing in common with the ordinary criminal, although there are also ordinary insane persons and criminals who, in given circumstances, sometimes perpetrate political attempts, as the effect of a kind of epidemic such as occurred in the religious attempts of the Middle Ages. But even when the political homicide is committed only through the impulsion of an honorable social ideal, the personal factor plays its part, as is sometimes seen in the case where the one selected to accomplish such an act is unable to overcome his repugnance to shedding blood and prefers suicide.

The same may be said of chance murder ("homicide occasionel") which is the consequence of gambling or drink. The proof of it is that not all of those who become drunk or dispute in gaming end by giving knife wounds, even in approximately similar exterior circumstances, or in circumstances in which the differences are at most slight and not proportionate to the varying result between these two extremes: at one extreme animated words, at the other murder. For every attempt, one may, in relation to every criminal, repeat the same observation concerning the individual influences of each of the particular factors, on each subject, at each moment of his life; and one may say generally that, according to the different categories of delicts and delinquents, against the person or against property, against morality or honor, the biological, physical, or social factors predominate differently in the effective determination of the delict.

What we have said of the natural genesis of crime may also be said of every other form of human activity, normal or abnormal. Thus, for instance, one cannot speak of the other great manifestations of social pathology such as insanity, suicide, alcoholism, or vagabondage, nor of the great manifestations of biological pathology of which heredity and contagion are two fundamental conditions of development, without thinking that they are the resultants of the combined action of anthropological factors (hereditary predisposition or momentary disposition of the individual), of physical factors (conditions of the telluric medium), and of social factors (conditions of family life, sensitive, nervous, and intellectual). In this connection it is strange that one of the most incisive of contemporary sociologists, Durkheim, excludes from the causality of suicide, the anthropological factors (heredity and psycho-pathological conditions) and the physical factors (such as the changes of the seasons), notwithstanding that the constantly increasing number of suicides in the hot months depends, for instance, on the debilitation and irritability of the nervous system produced by excessive heat. One should not, however, disregard his explanation, although in itself insufficient, wherein he adverts to the greater length of the days and consequently the greater number of affairs and preoccupations in which the persons predisposed to suicide live.

Social Abnormality of Economics as Basis of Origin and Nature of Delinquency. Now these considerations on the inseparable concurrence of the anthropological, physical, and social factors in every form of human activity and on the variable importance of each of them in every particular case, not only assist us to develop and give precision to our idea on the origin and nature of criminality but they are useful as well in showing the insufficiency of the other group of hypotheses which are still to be examined. According to many of our critics, and especially those who have rarely or never studied criminals with a truly scientific method and by direct observation, criminality is a phenomenon of exclusively social origin, while showing one or another of the particular aspects which this kind of causes may take. There are some who maintain that the whole social medium is determined by economic conditions, and that consequently crime, in whatever form it presents itself, is but the effect of economic disease. I have so fully discussed this opinion elsewhere that there is no need of repetition here. The Marxian doctrine of historical materialism, which I think it more accurate to call the doctrine of *economic determinism,* according to which the economic conditions of each social group in each phase of its evolution determine, "in the last analysis," as Engel says, that is, directly or indirectly, both the moral sentiments and the political and legal institutions of the same group, is profoundly true. It is the fundamental law of positivistic sociology. Yet I think that this theory should be supplemented by admitting in the first place that the economic conditions of each people are in turn the natural resultant of its racial energies which unfold in a given telluric medium; and by admitting in the second place that the moral sentiments, ideas, and political and legal institutions also have their own relatively autonomous existence, *i.e.* within the limits of the variations of a given economic constitution on which they also have their more or less superficial reaction but which are nevertheless worthy of being noticed.

Social Abnormality of Juridical Inadaptation as Basis of Origin and Nature of Delinquency. A view has recently been urged which is in part a repetition of the accurate and well-known idea that the insane, the defectives, and the criminals, are beings relatively or absolutely unfit for social life and which is in part an evident derivation from the Marxian doctrines on the struggle of the classes for economic, and, hence, for political, supremacy. This view is that the delinquent is nothing other than an individual who has not known how or who has not been able to adapt himself to the penal laws which look to the defense of the interest of the dominant class at each historical moment. And this defect of adaptation ends in either direct revolt or in the degeneracy of individuals condemned to an inferior life. It will be more appropriate to speak of this opinion in treating of penal justice and social defense. It will here suffice to call attention to the inadmissible omission of the biological factor, since I can here again repeat: How does it happen that of a hundred individuals who are "nonadapted, or degenerate because of lack of adaptation to the juridical organization," only ten commit crimes while the others commit suicide or become insane? Further, of what use is this hypothesis, when there is a question of crimes which are not directed against the politico-social organization or which are committed to the prejudice, not of the dominant classes, but of the class of the delinquents? And finally, when the penal code punishes homicide and assault without distinction of persons, for instance, where the delinquent and his victim are both paupers, how can it be said that it protects only or preferentially the interests of the dominant class?

Social Abnormality of Complex Social Influences as Basis of Origin and Nature of Delinquency. I consider the opinion inaccurate and prejudiced which holds that crime is the exclusive or even the principal effect of social environment. Tarde sums it up by saying: "A given social organization, a given criminality." This opinion, originated by the Italians, then taken up by the French and more recently also by the Germans, without any new syllogistic argument and with a complete absence of observation of delinquents and the determinant causes of their anti-social existence, however, has appeared very seductive, not only because of its generality but also because it escapes, they claim, the fatalism of the anthropological social school. In effect, they say, if crime is but the exclusive effect of atavism and pathology, society can do little or nothing to reduce its intensity and extension. On the contrary, in affirming that crime is essentially a social phenomenon, there is also affirmed the comforting possibility of reducing or even eliminating it by improving or changing social conditions. The opinion is accurate in itself, but there is no justification for opposing it to the positivist criminal school, which has never, even through its most specially anthropological representatives, asserted that crime is always and solely a biological phenomenon.

Biologico-Social Abnormality as Basis of Origin and Nature of Delinquency. Yet, aside from this, it is evident that this idea does not explain all the forms of delict and all the categories of delinquents. It considers too exclusively chance criminality ("criminalité occasionelle") in which we ourselves from the very beginning have always maintained the predominance of the social factors. A sufficient proof of this is our theory of the equivalents for penalty, which we will take up at a later point. This oft-repeated affirmation puts the question badly and the solution is still worse. It is the same as if one were to ask whether the air or the lung contributed most to the life of a mammal. They both contribute and that is the whole truth.

Let us not be told that, admitting this, the social factors are always the real and first causes, because it is from them that individual organic and psychic anomalies and degeneration are derived by hereditary transmission: this would be a Byzantine quibble like the discussion of the priority of the egg or the hen. In the indissolubility and infinite complexity of natural causes and effect, it is an illusory pretension to wish to find first causes, since it is certain that every cause is also an effect and every effect in turn becomes a cause. Moreover, bearing in mind what I have said above; namely, that economic and social conditions are, in their turn, a resultant of racial energies in a given telluric medium, and that there is a relatively autonomous development of each order of social facts in the field of economic conditions,—one sees that it is more positivistic to admit and define by scientific observations the respective and concomitant influences of the different factors of crime, were it only because this bio-sociological diagnosis of crime does not take anything away from the truth of the socialistic prognosis, according to which, in a quite different economic and social environment, wherein every human being would be assured really human conditions of life and, hence, the development of his personality, the epidemic sources of crime would be dammed up, eliminating degeneracy through poverty in the masses and degeneracy through parasitism in the few.

Crime is a Phenomenon of Biologico-Social Abnormality. Hence, in conclusion, we return to our fundamental assertion which should control not only criminal anthropology but all the inductions of criminal sociology: that crime, like all other human acts, is a phenomenon of complex origin, both biological and physio-social, with different modalities and degrees according to the different circumstances of persons and things, of times and places.

We have a last observation to make in this connection. Colajanni thought he struck a fearful blow at the theory of anthropological factors in crime, by establishing (but with many grave errors which I have pointed out in my Italian editions) that "the criminality of a region in Italy is deployed in the inverse ratio to organic degeneracy." In similar fashion, Durkheim, in order to deny that the psychopathic conditions of the individual are among the causes of suicide, remarks that the frequency of suicide is in inverse ratio to that of insanity. Now both of these observed facts, to the extent that they are true, are explicable by the law of compensation between both forms of psychopathic condition. The pathological or degenerative condition which shows itself by crime does not show itself under other forms; or vice versa, if it manifests itself by suicide or insanity or ordinary disease, it in that way eliminates the sources of criminality. Goethe has expressed this in an admirable synthesis which applies alike to individuals and to the population of a whole region and to the collectivity of each social class. He says: "Since the budget of Nature is limited, if she expends too much energy in one direction, she economizes in another."

We have thus finished the examination of the principal objections which, in a more or less positivistic or scientific field, have been urged against the method, the foundation, and the principal data of criminal anthropology. We may therefore conclude that, apart from the inevitable partial corrections, none of the criticisms made is able to take from the data of criminal anthropology that value which it is quite capable of demonstrating by facts while progressing and becoming more perfect every day: and this, in spite of all the criticisms of pure ratiocination, proves that it is advancing, notwithstanding inaccuracies and partial errors, along the great highway of positivistic and fruitful truth. Onesidedness is the organic defect of all the objections made to the data of criminal anthropology. The critics have always wished to assume, for the convenience of controversy, that the new science considers crime as a solely and exclusively biological phenomenon; whereas, from the beginning, its founders, while provisionally separating for exigent reasons of study this or that side of the criminal phenomenon, have nevertheless always affirmed its complex natural determination, both in the biological order and in the physical and social orders. Criminal sociology is inseparable from criminal biology; and such, affirmatively, is the last result of our study.

NATURAL CLASSIFICATION OF CRIMINALS

Five Categories of Criminals. Having demonstrated by means of anthropology and statistics the reality of this basic distinction between habitual and occasional delinquents of which so many observers had already an intuition, but which had as yet taken no definite form, we have established the starting-point for those successive distinctions which the study of facts led me to introduce into criminal science and which have since been accepted under more or less different names by all experts in criminal sociology.

These ulterior distinctions are determined by the criteria of fact which follow. First of all in the mass of habitual delinquents there are presented those who are affected with an obvious and clinical form of mental alienation from which proceeds their criminal activity. In the second place, among the habitual delinquents who are not mentally affected, little as one may have visited the prisons and studied delinquents from the sociological standpoint, one finds a class of individuals physically and morally ill-favored from birth, who live in crime by reason of a congenital necessity of organic and psychic adaptation, and who are closer to insanity than to normal reason. This category is distinguished from another class of individuals who also live in crime and by crime owing to the predominant influence of the social environment in which they were born and have grown up,—an influence always found together with a wretched organic and psychic constitution. These individuals, however, once having reached the state of chronic crime, are incorrigible and degenerate like the other habitual criminals; but, before the descent from the first crime to the depths, they could easily have been saved by preventive institutions and by a medium less profoundly vicious.

Moreover, in the class of occasional delinquents a special category is distinguished, less by different characteristics than by the typical exaggeration of its organic and psychic characteristics hence, almost exclusively by differences in degree—greater or less. In all of these individuals it is rather the impulsion of occasion than innate tendency which determines the crime. With the majority the determining occasion is a quite common, or, at least, a not too exceptional stimulus,— but for some, on the contrary, the stimulus is an outburst of extraordinary passion, a psychological tempest which of itself can carry them to the point of crime. Some of these individuals are normal men; others who, so to speak, complete the circle are in a class, as Delbruck, and Baer have said, which is closely related to that of the criminal insane, if not with a permanent form of derangement at least with a lack of psychic equilibrium, which, at first more or less latent, finally breaks out in a criminal attempt.

The whole mass of delinquents classify themselves into five categories which as early as 1880 I designated as follows: Criminal-insane— criminal-born—habitual criminals or criminals by acquired habit— chance criminals ("d'occasion")—criminals by passion.

The Criminal Insane. As I have already said, criminal anthropology will not have reached its definite phase until it shall advance by biological, psychological, and statistical biographies in each of these categories, giving to each in a qualitative and quantitative way psychological characteristics with a greater precision than now obtains, since the present observers give characteristics for a whole mass of delinquents who are distinguished only by the legal form of the crime committed and not according to their bio-social type as well. In the works of Lombroso, Marro, and others and even in my "Omicidio" to a considerable extent, the characteristics are indicated either for the total or else according to the legal categories of delinquents (murderers, thieves, forgers, etc.), in each of which categories there are born-criminals, habitual criminals, occasional or chance criminals, and insane criminals. It follows that there are either partial disagreements between observers, or at least a kind of average in the characteristics of each anthropological class of criminals. Now, in consequence of the studies that have been made and especially since my studies on hundreds of delinquents, ordinary madmen, and normal persons, we are able to point out here the general lines which distinguish these five anthropological classes of delinquents. First, it is evident that in a classification of delinquents which does not limit itself exclusively to the technical field of criminal anthropology and which must afford a positive base for the inductions of criminal sociology, the category of the *criminal insane* is fully entitled to a place. There is no necessity to be long with the objection that Joly has again recently made me, wherein he claims that the term—criminal-insane—is a contradiction of terms because the insane are not criminal as they lack moral responsibility. I shall make reply to this assertion, which is inspired by the traditional spiritualism, in treating of social accountability which applies even to the criminal insane. In the meantime, when speaking of insane persons who commit some of those acts which if committed by sane men would be called crimes, we shall consider the term in its objective sense which is not open to discussion. Nor should we halt on the objection made by Bianchi, among others, at the Criminal Anthropology Congress of Rome; namely, that the criminal insane belong to psychiatry. The fact that psychiatry is concerned with them from the standpoint of psychopathology does not prevent criminal anthropology and criminal sociology from being occupied with them, either in every form of natural study of the criminal, or in indicating measures concerning them in the interest of public safety. Among the criminal insane there is a whole variety, recognized since the studies of Lombroso and since the quasi-unanimity of the Italian psychiatrists shown at the Phreniatrical Congress of Sienna, which is not distinguishable from that of real born-criminals. These are the morally insane afflicted with the hitherto little-defined phrenopathic form to which science has given so many names, from "moral imbecility," used by Pritchard, to "reasoning insanity," employed by Verga. This mental infirmity, which has been recently studied, especially in the works of Mendel, Degrand du Saulle, Maudsley, Krafft-Ebing, Savage Hugues, Hollander, Bonfigli, Tamburini and Seppilli, Bonnecchiato, G. B. Verga, Salemi, Pace, Bleuler, Barr, Waggoner, and others, consists in the last analysis in the absence or atrophy of the moral sense (which I prefer to call the social sense of what is permitted or forbidden). It is most often congenital but sometimes acquired. It coexists with apparent integrity of logical reasoning and presents the fundamental psychological condition of the born-criminal. This is an observation of the greatest importance in avoiding the easy misapprehensions into which certain critics of the positive school have fallen. In failing to note the absolute difference between the morally insane and ordinary madmen they have revolted against a pretended "identification between criminals and madmen" which has never had any place in the inductions of criminal anthropology. Aside from morally insane persons who are indeed rare and who, as Lombroso and Krafft-Ebing remark, are more often sent to prison as delinquents than to special houses as patients, there is a whole phalanx of unfortunates who are afflicted with a common and more or less apparent form of mental infirmity. In this pathological state they commit crimes sometimes atrocious in the cases for instance of idiocy, the mania of persecution, violent mania, epilepsy, or in attempts against property and morals; also in cases of general paralysis, epilepsy, and imbecility. A general description of these numerous and very different kinds of insane cannot be given here because their organic and especially psycho-pathological characteristics are not only at the same time identical and opposed to those of non-insane criminals, but also, and especially, because these characteristics often vary with the different forms of mental malady and hence, as Lombroso also thinks, they cannot be gathered into a single type as can be done for the other categories of delinquents.

The Mattoide and Semi-insane Categories. Besides the really insane, who are, as I have pointed out and been confirmed by others, only an exaggeration of the born criminal type, this category also embraces the delinquents who are neither completely sane nor insane and belong to what Maudsley called the "intermediate zone." Lombroso denotes them with the term "mattoides" which is now part of ordinary language since it expresses in a popular untechnical form an indisputable fact. It is really a mere prejudice to believe that there are found in nature the precise distinctions to which human language is forced to resort and that, for instance, in the present case there is a clean-cut difference between the sane and the insane. No, there is a shading of tints where we pass from one to the other by transitions which are difficult of determination. Types of these half-insane delinquents are afforded us by those who finish their existence with a crime, often political in character or appearance. Their lives have been full of extravagances which are often characteristically expressed in a mania for writing and publishing a flood of pamphlets, wherein, in spite of only the most rudimentary education, they treat of the highest topics. Such are the Lazzarettis, the Magiones, the Passanantes, the Guiteaus, the Macleans, etc. It is the half-insane who commit the most atrocious and repelling crimes of bloodshed with a coolness which proceeds from their pathological organization, and without any apparent motive or without a motive proportionate to its effect. And yet the classical criminalists find in them the maximum of "moral liberty" and of responsibility when they speak of homicides committed "without cause" or simply through "brutal perversity" or through a sort of "sanguinary erotism" or through "hatred for humanity." We find other examples among those whom alienists call necrophilo-maniacs who are equally impelled to murder or rape—like that Sergeant Bertrand who dug up bodies to violate them,—or Verzeni who violated women after having strangled them,—or Menesclou who was sentenced to death at Paris for hacking to pieces a little girl of seven after he had violated her.

Finally, a large contingent is furnished to this category by those who are afflicted with hereditary insanity and epilepsy, under forms of these maladies which are much more frequent than is generally believed, and to which the latest results of psychopathology reduce the greater part of those strange forms of alienation that were formerly called temporary insanity and in which various kinds of monomania are observed. One of these latter, "misdéisme," deserves mention. It is the kind of homicide with the massacre of several persons, committed generally by soldiers on their comrades or their superiors, without any apparent serious motive. This is certainly an expression of epilepsy among individuals whom a more careful and a more rigorous examination before enlistment would have kept out of the service, and would avoid the frequent repetition of these tragedies, which it is absurd, as well as useless, to persist in combating with the death penalty. In this connection we should recall that Lombroso, although at first identifying moral insanity with congenital delinquency, finally traced both to epilepsy, making, as I had already declared, the epileptoid constitution the common base of all forms of delinquency. Certainly the positive proofs advanced by him are so numerous and agree so well that after the first objections, which were inevitable and which were made also to the assimilation of the morally insane with the born criminal, this view will finally be definitely conceded, or, at least essentially. Already in practice it seems to explain certain strange and savage crimes wherein one very often finds traces of the epileptic temperament of which formerly one never thought except in the most pronounced and rarest cases.

The Born-Criminal Category. Finally comes the category of the *criminal-born* which is, properly-speaking, made up of those in whom there is observed clearly the special marks revealed by criminal anthropology. These are the types of men, either savage and brutal or polished and idle, who are unable to distinguish murder, robbery, and crime in general from honest industry. They are "delinquents just as others are good workmen"; and have ideas and sentiments on crime and punishment entirely opposed to those which legislators and criminologists think they have. With these delinquents, a penalty suffered has, as Romagnosi said, less effect than a penalty which threatens. It has, in fact, none at all because they consider prison as a refuge where food is assured them even in winter without need of much labor and more often with enforced idleness; or, at the most, as a risk inseparable from their criminal industry, just like any other risk, such as falling from a false work which is incurred by a mason or the risks incurred by railway servants.

These with the habitual delinquents constitute, under the two characteristic and opposed types of murderers and thieves, the phalanx of those who, scarcely released from prison, again commit crime and are eternal pensioners of all the houses of detention. Well known to police and the courts, they count their convictions for trifling offenses by the dozen or more. Against these, the legislator, closing his eyes to daily experience, persists in the useless and costly fight between penalties which cause no fear and delicts ceaselessly repeated. The idea of a born-criminal (who is criminal by the inexorable tyranny of congenital tendencies) is certainly contrary to common opinion, which insists that every man should impute his conduct to his free will or at most to a defective and badly directed training rather than to the ordinary composition of his organic and physical constitution. It thus lends itself to facile and oratorical contradictions. Further, the incompetents who visit the prisons are unable either to find or see these types of delinquents; and this is partly, as l'Abbé Crozès (who observed and knew the prison world to the very bottom) has very well shown. He says: "these incorrigibles are ordinarily inoffensive and often useful prisoners, and have only the best relations with the keepers and directors, who say of them: 'He is a good prisoner who listens to reason, and would not harm a fly.' Prison life is no suffering for them: they are there like the painter in his studio where he thinks of new master-pieces." But this same common opinion when it is not preoccupied with the dreadful and imaginary consequences of the irresponsibility for crime committed under such conditions, recognizes, at least in the evident cases, that there are men born for crime whose anti-human conduct is the inevitable effect of an indefinite series of hereditary influences which accumulate in the course of generations. This is proven by the success which has attended in ordinary language my expression, the *born-criminal*. Science, moreover, to which in the end the common opinion surrenders, has gathered such convincing proofs of this idea; practical life has so confirmed it with the general testimony of prison directors and prison doctors, that the fact will surely be impressed upon legislators, unless they wish to imitate the hen which after hatching ducklings, undertook to correct them of their innate desire to swim by pecking them every time they came out of the water,—a process which did not prevent their immediate return in spite of her.

The Habitual Delinquent Category. In the third place is the category of delinquents whom, as the result of studies principally made in the prisons, I have called habitual delinquents or delinquents by acquired habit. These individuals show in an indistinct way, if at all, the anthropological marks of the born-criminal. The first crime is committed very often at a tender age and almost always against property and less through innate tendencies than through the moral weakness peculiar to them, to which is added the impulsion of circumstances and a corrupt environment which constitute a true center of criminal infection. Often, also, as Joly observes, they are encouraged by the impunity following their first faults and persist in crime, which then becomes a chronic habit and a real profession. This comes from the fact that detention in common corrupts them morally and physically, confinement in cells stupifies them, alcoholism brutalizes them, and society, abandoning them after as before their liberation, to wretchedness, idleness, and temptation, does not help them in their struggle to re-enter the conditions of honest life. "Society may even have forced them to fall back into crime by certain institutions such as segregation, admonition, and surveillance, which ought to be preventive but which, on the contrary, are new causes of crime." Adults and even youths are sentenced ten, twenty, and thirty times to short terms, generally for theft or vagabondage, and this simply because after their first crime, admonition and surveillance together with the corruption of the so-called houses of correction and prisons deprived them of every means of honestly gaining their living. Judges and lawyers know it well. They know that with these badly combined social mechanisms, Thomas Moore was right in saying "What are you doing but making thieves in order to have the pleasure of putting them in prison?" It is precisely the thieves that in my opinion form, together with other similar delinquents against property, the principal contingent of delinquents by acquired habit, because trained or forced to begging and to theft from their tender infancy by their families or by other persons who, especially in large cities, become promoters and professors of crime, they do not know honest toil and are the "bedouins" of the great cities.

The Criminal through Passion Category. In addition to the categories of which we have just spoken there remain the last two: criminals through passion and criminals by occasion (chance criminals). Criminals through excess of passion ("delinquenti per impeto di passione"), who form a more distinct variety of occasional criminals, show certain characteristics which easily distinguish them. According to Lombroso, who even in his second edition supplementing Despine and Bittenger, gave a really complete list, we are able to say first of all that these criminals who show especially the type of "irresistible impulse" commit crimes against the person and are quite rare. Thus, of seventy-one criminals through passion studied by Lombroso, sixty-nine were guilty of either homicide or assault; six had been convicted of robbery; three of arson and one of rape. As to their number, Lombroso, like Bittinger and Guillaume, asserted that criminals through passion number five per cent. of the total. This figure is certainly exaggerated. In the first place, Guillaume says that crimes committed through passion furnish five per cent. Not of convicts in general but of persons convicted through correctional channels. Bittinger makes a general comparison between the crimes through passion and those committed on reflection, which is seemingly very different from Lombroso's comparison of delinquents through passion with habitual delinquents. In fact, we know that real delinquents through an excess of passion are for the most part homicidal. When we observe that the total number of murders, including manslaughter, in Italy is scarcely four per cent. of the whole number of convicts of every kind, and in France 0.3 per cent., we see clearly that delinquents through passion cannot constitute five per cent. of the total. In the type which is peculiar to them, they scarcely furnish five per cent. of the sanguinary crime. In fact, this correction was adopted by Lombroso in his fifth edition. These are the individuals whose lives have previously been blameless—men of a sanguine or nervous temperament with exaggerated sensibility, quite the reverse of the born and habitual criminals. They are sometimes of a temperament closely related to that of the insane or epileptic, of which their criminal rage may be only a disguised manifestation. Most often (especially in the case of women) they commit the crime in their youth under the impulse of uncontrolled passion, like anger, jealousy, or shame. Their emotion is violent before, during, and after the crime, which is not committed secretly or stealthily but openly and often by ill-chosen means, the first which come to hand. There are sometimes, however, criminals through passion who premeditate and cunningly execute a crime either because of a less impulsive temperament or, in the cases of endemic crime, under the influence of prejudices and public opinion. That is why in criminal psychology premeditation has no absolute value in distinguishing the born-criminal from the criminal through passion; for premeditation depends more upon individual temperament than upon anything else, and is found equally in crimes committed by all the anthropological types. Among the other characteristics peculiar to criminals through passion is the fact that the determinant psychological cause is proportionate to the crime and that the crime (I must add) is its own object and not a means to the commission of other crimes. They do not hesitate to avow their misdeed, and their excessive repentance may lead to suicide. In fact many commit suicide immediately or a short time after the criminal attack. If they are convicted (which rarely happens) they continue to show repentance and improve, or rather they are not corrupted in prison, thus affording a small number of obvious cases from which some observers believe themselves warranted in drawing the conclusion that the improvement of offenders is constant. On the contrary, however, improvement is unknown among born and habitual criminals. Criminals through passion show few or none of the characteristics, such as I have given in studying the physiognomies of homicides. These are the distinctions of the criminal by excess of passion. They are, however, less marked in countries where certain crimes against the person are endemic, such as homicide for revenge or on a point of honor in Corsica and Sardinia, or the political homicides of a few years ago in Russia and Ireland.

The Occasional Criminal Category. There is finally the category of occasional criminals ("delinquenti d'occasione"). These chance criminals have not received from nature an active tendency towards crime but have fallen into it, goaded by the temptation incident to their personal condition or physical and social environment and who do not repeat their offense if these temptations are removed. They commit crimes, therefore, which do not belong to natural delinquency, and even in the commission of crimes against the person or property they act under individual and social conditions entirely different from those in which such crimes are committed by born criminals and habitual delinquents. Assuredly, even in the chance criminal, a part of the causes which determine the crime belong to the anthropological order; since, without the particular dispositions of the individual, the exterior impulsions would be insufficient. For example, in a period of hard times the whole population does not devote itself to theft. One man prefers the sufferings of honest and undeserved poverty, another goes so far as to beg; and even among those who descend to crime, some are content with larceny, while others commit burglary or highway robbery. But since there are no absolute distinctions in nature, the fundamental difference between the chance criminal and the born-criminal consists always in this fact, that in the latter the external stimulus is secondary when compared to the internal criminal tendency which in itself has a centrifugal force impelling the individual to crime; while in the former is found rather a feebleness of resistance to external stimulus, which consequently becomes the principal determinant force. The incident which provokes the crime in the case of the born-criminal is simply the point of application of a preëxisting instinct, so to speak. It is less an occasion than a pretext. With the occasional criminal it is, on the contrary, the real stimulus which vitalizes the latent criminal spark. In the born-criminal it is a fact which determines the discharge of a persistent distinctive force; in the chance criminal it is a fact which simultaneously causes the growth and explosion of a criminal instinct. For this reason Lombroso calls occasional delinquents, criminaloids ("criminaloidi") to indicate that their organic and psychic constitution presents abnormality, in lesser degree than is found in true criminals or born-criminals. The relation expressed is analogous to those shown by the words metal and metaloid or epileptic and epileptoid. Such a definition, however, destroys the criticisms that Lombroso himself made of the idea of the occasional criminal category when he said, as did Benedikt at the Congress of Rome and as Sergi has later repeated, that "all criminals are born-criminals," and hence the true occasional criminal or the normal man, urged to crime by occasion alone, does not exist. For my part, in accord with Garofalo, even in the second edition of this work (1884), I have never expressed any such conception of the occasional criminal. But on the contrary I have always said, as Lombroso himself admits a little farther on, quoting my words, that there is only a difference of degree and modality between the born and the occasional criminal,—a thing, moreover, which is true of all the categories of delinquents. Of the two conditions which psychologically determine crime—moral insensibility and lack of foresight ("improvidenza")—the crime of occasion is traceable to the latter, while congenital and habitual delinquency is principally traceable to the former. In the born-criminal it is lack of social feeling which prevents him from recoiling before crime. In the occasional criminal this social sense exists or is much less obtuse, and not being seconded by a sufficiently lively appreciation of the consequences, it yields to the exterior impulsion, without which it was strong enough and would have remained strong enough to hold the individual in the straight path. In every man, no matter how pure and honest he may be, the fugitive thought of a dishonest or criminal act occurs on certain seductive occasions. But in the honest man, because of his organic and moral fiber, this tempting image which immediately awakens a vivid idea of the possible consequences is overcome by his strong psychic organization. With a man of less strength and less foresight it overpowers the resistance of a weak moral sense and finally conquers, because, as Victor Hugo says, "in the face of duty, doubt is defeat." A criminal by passion is a man with sufficient strength to resist ordinary and mild temptations but without sufficient force to resist the psychological tempest which sometimes becomes so violent that no man, be he ever so strong, could resist it. The forms of occasional delinquency that we have enumerated contain the reason for their origin, in the accidental character which distinguishes them. Following Lombroso, the general stimulants of age, sexuality, poverty, influence of the weather, of the moral environment, of alcoholism, of personal circumstances, and of imitation (of which Tarde has undoubtedly exaggerated the casual importance in social facts but showing fully the part which they play in human activity) must be taken into consideration. Thus Lombroso distinguishes two varieties of occasional criminals: on the one hand, the pseudo-criminals, *i.e.,* normal men who commit involuntary crimes, political crimes, or misdeeds which imply no perversity and involve no damage to society, although the law considers them criminal; on the other hand, the criminaloids, who commit ordinary crimes but who are differentiated from ordinary criminals for the reasons above given.

Difference Between Categories One of Degree. Apropos of these anthropological categories, we would make a last general observation—one which meets certain objections frequently made by those syllogistic critics of criminal anthropology who have never personally observed nor studied criminals. In the first place, the differences between these five classes of criminals are only differences of degree and modality, both in their organic and psychic traits and in the concurrence of the physical and social environment. There is no essential difference between the groups of any natural classification. This is not only true of mineralogy, botany, zoölogy, or general anthropology, but of criminal anthropology as well. It does not take away either experimental solidity or practical importance from the natural classification. The same is true of the classifications of criminal anthropology. In natural history we pass by degrees and shades from the inorganic world to the organic (since even in minerals there is a minimum degree and a first form of life as is shown by the laws of crystallization), and biology is only an ulterior evolution of physics and chemistry. In the organic world we pass by degrees and shades from proteids to vegetation, then to animals and their species which become more diversified as they multiply. So, also, in criminal anthropology, we pass gradually from the insane criminal to the born-criminal passing over the morally insane and epileptic delinquents. From the born-criminal we pass to the occasional criminal meeting on the road the criminal by acquired habit who begins as an occasional wrongdoer and finally ends, through acquired degeneracy, in showing the organic characteristics and especially the psychic traits of the born-criminal. Finally, we pass from the occasional criminal to the criminal by passion who is of a more distinct variety, since, with his neurotic, hysterical, or epileptoid or mattoid temperament, the criminal by passion often resembles or is partly merged in the insane criminal.

WILLEM ADRIAAN BONGER
(1876–1940)

The events surrounding Bonger's birth hardly equal the dramatic tragedy of his death. His father was in the insurance business in Amsterdam; his mother was an amiable housewife. Both had assured Willem the comforts of a large family by having nine children before him.

Willem attended the Gymnasium and thereafter the University of Amsterdam as a student of law. While at university he encountered two influences which were decisive in shaping his later professional life. First, he joined with a number of other students interested in socialism; and, second, he came under the influence of his professor of criminal law, the renowned G. A. van Hamel whose interest in criminal science included not only the law but also the behavioral sciences, especially anthropology and sociology.

At one point in his university career, Bonger competed for a prize in an essay contest on the subject, "Un aperçu systematique et critique de la litterature concernant l'influence des conditions économique sur la criminalité." He didn't win the first prize, but his essay together with his doctoral dissertation on the same subject make up his major work, Criminalité et Conditions Économique.

Bonger shared with his spiritual predecessor, Karl Marx, an empassioned sympathy for the earth's downtrodden together with monumental energy and precision in marshalling and presenting evidence describing their plight. Criminality and Economic Conditions *is at one and the same time a masterful analysis and a devastating critique of the capitalist system and the criminogenic conditions Bonger saw inherent therein.*

Though not a pacifist, Bonger was appalled by the inhumanity of war and spoke out loudly against the growing spectre of Nazism. When German troops invaded Holland in 1940, he refused to leave the country, but—knowing his previous anti-Nazi activities had sealed his fate in his homeland, he took his own life.

WILLEM ADRIAAN BONGER

Criminality and Economic Conditions

THE NATURE OF CRIME

A crime is an act committed within a group of persons that form a social unit, and whose author is punished by the group (or a part of it) as such, or by organs designated for this purpose, and this by a penalty whose nature is considered to be more severe than that of moral disapprobation. This definition, however, considers only the formal side of the conception of crime; it says nothing as to its essence. It is proper, then, to consider next the material side.

Crime is an act. The question which presents itself first of all is this: Is crime considered from a biological point of view an abnormal act? The answer to this, which is of the highest importance for the etiology of crime, must be negative. From a biological point of view almost all crimes must be ranked as normal acts. The process which takes place in the brain of the gendarme when he kills a poacher who resists arrest is identical with that which takes place in the brain of the poacher killing the gendarme who pursues him. It is only the social environment which classes the second act rather than the first as a crime. From the biological point of view homicide is not an abnormal act. Sociology and history prove that men have always killed when they thought it necessary. No one would maintain, for example, that those who take part in a war are biologically abnormal.

Continuing our researches into the essence of crime, it is obvious that it is an immoral act, and one of a serious character. And in treating the matter thus we observe that the acts called immoral are those which are harmful to the interests of a group of persons united by the same interests. Since the social structure is changing continually, the ideas of what is immoral (and consequently of what is or is not criminal) change with these modifications.

Considered in this way from the material side, a crime is an anti-social act, an act which is harmful in a considerable degree to the interests of a certain group of persons. This definition is not yet complete, however, for many acts of this nature are not crimes.

It is clear that what must be added to our definition (already contained implicitly in the formal definition) is that the act must be prejudicial to the interests of those who have the power at their command. Power then is the necessary condition for those who wish to class a certain act as a crime.

It follows that in every society which is divided into a ruling class and a class ruled, penal law has been principally constituted according to the will of the former. We must at once add that the present legal prescriptions are not always directed against the class of those ruled, but that most of them are directed against acts that are prejudicial to the interests of both classes equally (for example, homicide, rape, etc.). These acts would without doubt continue to be considered criminal if the power were to pass into the hands of those who are at present the governed. However, in every existing penal code hardly any act is punished if it does not injure the interests of the dominant class as well as the other, and the law touching it protects only the interests of the class dominated. The rare exceptions are explained by the fact that the lower classes are not wholly without power.

This is our conclusion, then, that a crime is an act committed within a group of persons forming a social unit; that it prejudices the interests of all, or of those of the group who are powerful; that, for this reason, the author of the crime is punished by the group (or a part of the group) as such or by specially ordained instruments, and this by a penalty more severe than moral disapprobation.

To find the causes of crime we must, then, first solve the question: "Why does an individal do acts injurious to the interests of those with whom he forms a social unit?", or in other words; "Why does a man act egoistically?"

THE ORIGIN OF EGOISTIC ACTS IN GENERAL

What are the causes of egoistic acts? How does it happen that one man does harm to another? The answers that have been given to this primeval question may be divided into two groups. The first group attributes the cause to the man himself, the second to his environment.

The great majority of persons who treat of this question settle it in favor of innate egoism. They are of the opinion that man is egoistic by nature and that environment can produce no change in this (this is implied in the Christian doctrine of original sin).

This theory is naturally of the highest importance for criminal science, and it becomes still more so from the fact that, according to Professor Lombroso, crime is a manifestation of atavism, that is, that some individuals present anew traits of character belonging to their very remote ancestors. The criminal would thus be a savage in our present society. We must therefore examine to see whether the said theory is correct.

We have only to consult one of the standard works on zoölogy to perceive that there is no basis in this science to uphold the theory.

Scores of pages might be filled with facts proving that the primitive peoples of all races and in all parts of the world were not only not egoistic in their relations with the people they lived among, but rather the contrary.

At the Fifth Congress of Criminal Anthropology Dr. Steinmetz, in speaking upon the explanation of crime by the hypothesis of atavism, says: "It is not at all probable that our true born-criminal resembles the normal savage. The former is characterized by his ferocious egoism, while the latter is nothing if not a devoted member of the group whose customs he respects and whose interests he defends; the savage is very tender toward the children whom the criminal abandons; the savage is only cruel toward the enemy, the criminal toward all the world."

Before speaking of the real causes of egoism and altruism it may be well to attempt to answer the question, Whence come these inexact ideas? It is not difficult, in my opinion, to explain how it comes about that many men believe that the "homo homini lupus" of Hobbes has been true always and everywhere. The adherents of this opinion have studied principally men who live under capitalism, or under civilization; their correct conclusion has been that egoism is the predominant characteristic of these men, and they have adopted the simplest explanation of the phenomenon and say that this trait is inborn.

If they had known the periods anterior to civilization, they would have noted that the "homo homini lupus" is an historical phenomenon applicable during a relatively short period, and that consequently it is impossible that egoism should be innate in man. However great have been the social modifications during the period of civilization, the principal aim of men has always been, and still is, to acquire personal wealth, and men still remain divided into classes, that is into groups whose economic interests are contrary. This is why an examination of the earlier periods is of such high importance for sociology.

An erroneous interpretation of the Darwinian theory has also contributed to bring about the strange notion of the eternal character of the struggle of all against all. Darwin himself maintains nothing of the sort. In his "Origin of Species" he says in the clearest terms that the struggle between the individuals of the same species does not at all happen in every species: "There must in every case be a struggle for existence, either one individual with another of the same species, or with the individuals of distinct species, or with the physical conditions of life."

How does it happen that some animal species are social while others are not? It is impossible to maintain with some authors that sociability increases according to the degree of development attained by the animal.

When we study the social species of animals we notice that the life in common is in general *one of their most powerful weapons in the struggle for existence,* a weapon without which it would be nearly or quite impossible for them to maintain the fight. Consequently the animals for which the life in common is advantageous and which possess social instincts stronger than others, have, when brought together by any cause whatever, a greater chance to survive. Per contra the animals who have to stalk their prey have more chance of surviving when life in common is disagreeable to them. It is therefore by survival that social feelings are developed in some species of animals and not in others. Habit, and the tendency to imitate increase these feelings considerably.

The advantages to certain species of animals resulting from life in common are of two kinds; in the first place a better defense against their enemies, and in the second place greater ease in procuring subsistence.

One of the principal characteristics of social animals is the pleasure they experience in living in common, so that a social animal is unhappy if he is separate from those of the group in which he lives. Further it is necessary that the animal that cannot live alone, and is happy with his group, should also feel a sympathy with that group. Pleasure or its opposite felt by any individual reacts upon the whole group. A social being will try then to favor the interests of his fellows as far as he can, and in so far as he comprehends these interests. This sympathy will not extend to the whole species but only to the group. The general interest of the group does not permit the sympathy to embrace the whole species, but on the contrary requires one group to fight the other if, for example, the latter interferes with its food-supply. And even within the limits of the group the general interest may demand that a sick or wounded individual be abandoned, when by its presence it would for example, attract beasts of prey, and thus put the existence of all in danger.

Highly developed sympathy produces the spirit of sacrifice, which impels the individual to assist his companions sometimes even at the risk of his life. This quality is reinforced by the desire of gaining the praise and avoiding the blame of companions, which desire in its turn is brought about only by the life in common. For the one that lives in conjunction with others, and takes pleasure in doing so, whose interests are those of the members of the group, must be sensible of the approval or disapproval of his acts felt by others, since their feelings of pleasure or displeasure react upon himself. The lack of the power of speech among animals, however, limits the force of praise or blame among them.

We come now to the question: what are the causes of altruism among men? It must be considered as certain that man has always lived in groups more or less large, and it is even very probable that he is descended from animals equally social. A study of the means man has of sustaining the struggle for existence proves that they are of such a nature that he would have succumbed if he had lived in isolation. Kautsky puts it thus: "... man ... whose mightiest and most effective, almost whose only weapon, indeed, in the struggle for existence, is association. He is, to be sure, distinguished above other animals by his intelligence, but this too is to the fruit of society, for in isolation he becomes dull and stupid. All man's other weapons in the struggle for existence are less efficient than those of the beasts. He has no weapons of attack like the beasts of prey, nor is he protected by his size like the elephant, hippopotamus and rhinoceros. He lacks the quickness of the squirrel and deer, and cannot repair his losses through superabundant fertility."

It is therefore on account of his constitution and of the struggle that he has had to sustain for his existence that man is a social being; in other words, those who showed social instincts stronger than the others ran less danger of succumbing in the contest for life, and had more chance of transmitting their leanings to their posterity. As man has greater intellectual capacities than the animals he is more capable of understanding the joys and sorrows of his fellows, and so is better able to assist the one and avoid the other. In the second place he has a developed language at his command, through which a great influence can be exercised upon conduct by blame and praise.

The fact that man is born with social instincts does not, however, explain altruism sufficiently, for among animal species there is not one whose individuals have done so much harm to one another as men, who, though they are social beings, are capable of committing the most egoistic acts. How shall we explain these contradictions?

We have seen above that primitive peoples, to whom we have referred showed very altruistic traits of character. The members of a group extend mutual aid, and, in their relations with one another, are benevolent, honest, truthful, and very susceptible to the opinions of others, etc.

It is impossible to explain this either by the race to which these peoples belong or by the climate in which they live, for they are of different races (for example North American Indians and the Hindoos of the delta of the Ganges) and live under different climates (as the Eskimos and the South American Indians). Besides this some of these peoples show towards strangers, qualities directly contrary to those they display toward members of their own group.

Consequently the cause can only be found in the social environment, which is determined in its turn by the mode of production. What follows will show that in the last instance it is the mode of production that is able to develop the social predisposition innate in man (not in the same measure for each individual, which is a question that I shall return to) or prevent this disposition from being developed, or may even destroy it entirely. Upon examining the modes of production in force among the peoples cited we see that they are characterized by the following traits, very different from those of the present system.

The first of these characteristic traits is this: *production takes place among these peoples for personal consumption and not for exchange as with us.*

The second characteristic of the modes of production of the peoples in question is bound up with the first, namely that *there was neither wealth nor poverty.* If there was privation (through scarcity of game, for example), all suffered; if there was abundance, all profited by it.

The third fact to be noted is that *the subordination of man to nature was very great,* so great that we, who have so largely subjugated the forces of nature, can have no idea of it. If primitive men were very weak in their contest with nature even when joined together in a single group, individually they were absolutely unable to maintain the struggle, and were thus forced to unite.

If we consider the characteristics of the primitive modes of production it becomes clear, it seems to me, why the primitive peoples were not more egoistic. They had neither rich nor poor; their economic interests were either parallel or equal (the latter in the case of production in common); the economic life, therefore, did not arouse egoistic ideas—they were not led into temptation. Where the economic system does not produce egoistic ideas it accustoms men to being unegoistic, and if their interests do happen occasionally to conflict, the matter is looked at altruistically and not egoistically. And since the economic life is the "conditio sine qua non" of life in general, and thus occupies the important place in human existence, it stamps the whole life with its non-egoistic character. Since the struggle for existence must be sustained in common against nature, if it is to be efficacious it binds human interests so closely together that they are inseparable; the interest of one is the same as that of his comrade.

We shall now understand why primitive men feel themselves to be first of all the members of a unit; why they not only abstain from acts harmful to their companions, but come to their aid whenever they can; why they are honest, benevolent, and truthful towards the members of their group, and why public opinion has so great an influence among them—characteristics which the quotations that I have already made have established. The cause of these facts is to be found in *the mode of production, which brought about a uniformity of interest in the persons united in a single group, obliged them to aid one another in the difficult and uninterrupted struggle for existence, and made men free and equal, since there was neither poverty nor riches, and consequently no possibility of oppression.*

The continual development of the productivity of labor has modified the structure of society greatly. As soon as productivity has increased to such an extent that the producer can regularly produce more than he needs, and the division of labor puts him in a position to exchange the surplus for things that he could not produce himself, at this moment there arises in man the notion of no longer giving to his comrades what they need, but of keeping for himself the surplus of what his labor produces, and exchanging it. Then it is that the mode of production begins to run counter to the social instincts of man instead of favoring it as heretofore.

However, this is only one side of the question. Through the development of exchange not only does man become egoistic towards those who for any reason are unable to provide for their needs, but exchange itself is an entirely egoistic act for the two parties who enter into it. Each tries to get as much profit for himself as possible, and consequently to make the other lose. The existence of economic laws which in many, and even in most cases prevent the two parties from injuring each other, does not change the fact at all. Commerce weakens the social instincts of man; the loss of one becomes the gain of another. When two persons are trading there springs up a tendency on the part of each to overvalue his own property and to disparage that of the other; commerce is one of the important causes of lying. In addition to this tendency another arises, that of giving goods of quality inferior to that agreed upon; the constant attention to one's own interests produces and develops fraud.

The more production for one's own use decreases, and the greater becomes the production for exchange, the more do habit and tradition produce in men the characteristics mentioned. As soon as exchange has developed to a certain point commerce begins to be a special trade. The merchant is much more exposed to the conditions named than those who trade only occasionally. Not only does he pass a great part of his life in exchanging but he is by profession egoistic in two directions; toward the producer from whom he buys, and toward the consumer to whom he sells.

When it reaches a certain height the continually increasing productivity of labor brings a further important modification in the social structure, namely slavery. For this springs up when production is so advanced that man can regularly produce more than he actually needs for himself, and when it is possible for him to exchange the overplus for things which he can use but cannot make. Prisoners of war are no longer killed as formerly, but are obliged to work for the profit of the conquerors. In this way is formed a considerable opposition of interest between two classes of individuals who together form a social unit: on the one hand those who, deprived of one of the most important factors of human happiness, liberty, are obliged to exhaust themselves for the benefit of others, and have only the strict necessaries of life; and on the other hand those who profit by the enslavement and excessive labor of the first.

Slavery (with the other forms of forced service, serfdom and wage-labor) is one of the most important factors that undermine the social instincts in man. Slavery, runs the saying, demoralizes the master as well as the slave. It arouses in the master the notion that the slave is not a thinking and feeling man like himself, but an instrument destined exclusively to be useful to him. In the slave himself it kills the feeling of independence; lacking the arms which the free man has at his disposal, the slave has recourse to dissimulation to defend himself against his master.

The overplus which one person can obtain by his own labor must always remain limited. Without the rise of slavery the great wealth of a single individual would not have been possible. To the difference between master and slave is now added that between rich and poor, and the envy and hatred of the poor for the rich, and the pride of the rich and their desire to dominate over the poor. Since the division of society into rich and poor the aristocracy has been formed, which does not owe its origin to the excellence of its members, as one might imagine from this inaccurate name, but to their wealth.

The period of civilization during which the social modification mentioned above has taken place is generally lauded to the skies, as compared with preceding epochs. In certain relations this is justifiable. Technique has made immense progress and especially during the last phase of civilization, capitalism; the power of man over nature has advanced greatly; the productivity of labor has been so increased that one class of men, exempted by this from permanent care for their daily bread, are able to devote themselves to the arts and sciences. All this is indisputable. But the development of the arts and sciences and of technique has only an indirect importance for the etiology of crime. The question first of all to be asked is this: What influence has this modification in the economic and social structure had upon the character of man? And the answer to this question can only be the following: this modification has engendered cupidity and ambition, has made man less sensitive to the happiness and misery of his fellows, and has decreased the influence exercised upon men's acts by the opinions of others. In short, it has developed egoism at the expense of altruism.

As we have seen in the preceding pages, it is certain that man is born with social instincts, which, when influenced by a favorable environment can exert a force great enough to prevent egoistic thoughts from leading to egoistic acts. And since crime constitutes a part of the egoistic acts, it is of importance, for the etiology of *crime in general,* to inquire whether the present method of production and its social consequences are an obstacle to the development of the social instincts, and in what measure. We shall try in the following pages to show the influence of the economic system and of these consequences upon the social instincts of man.

After what we have just said it is almost superfluous to remark that the egoistic tendency does not *by itself* make a man a criminal. For this something else is necessary. It is possible for the environment to create a great egoist, but this does not imply that the egoist will necessarily become criminal. For example, a man who is enriched by the exploitation of children may nevertheless remain all his life an honest man from the legal point of view. He does not think of stealing, because he has a surer and more lucrative means of getting wealth, although he lacks the moral sense which would prevent him from committing a crime if the thought of it occurred to him. We shall show that, as a consequence of the present environment, man has become very egoistic and hence more *capable of crime,* than if the environment had developed the germs of altruism.

The present economic system is based upon exchange. As we saw at the end of the preceding section such a mode of production cannot fail to have an egoistic character. A society based upon exchange isolates the individuals by weakening the bond that unites them. When it is a question of exchange the two parties interested think only of their own advantage even to the detriment of the other party. In the second place the possibility of exchange arouses in a man the thought of the possibility of converting the surplus of his labor into things which increase his well-being in place of giving the benefit of it to those who are deprived of the necessaries of life. Hence the possibility of exchange gives birth to cupidity.

The exchange called simple circulation of commodities is practiced by all men as consumers, and by the workers besides as vendors of their labor power. However, the influence of this simple circulation of commodities is weak compared with that exercised by capitalistic exchange. It is only the exchange of the surplus of labor, by the producer, for other commodities, and hence is for him a secondary matter. As a result he does not exchange with a view to profit, (though he tries to make as advantageous a trade as possible) but to get things which he cannot produce himself.

Capitalistic exchange, on the other hand, has another aim—that of making a profit. A merchant, for example, does not buy goods for his own use, but to sell them to advantage. He will, then, always try, on the one hand, to buy the best commodities as cheaply as possible, by depreciating them as much as he can; on the other hand, to make the purchaser pay as high a price as possible, by exaggerating the value of his wares. *By the nature of the mode of production itself* the merchant is therefore forced to make war upon two sides, must maintain his own interests against the interests of those with whom he does business. If he does not injure too greatly the interests of those from whom he buys, and those to whom he sells, it is for the simple reason that these would otherwise do business with those of his competitors who do not find their interest in fleecing their customers. Wherever competition is eliminated for whatever cause the tactics of the merchant are shown in their true light; he thinks only of his own advantage even to the detriment of those with whom he does business. "No commerce without trickery" is a proverbial expression (among consumers), and with the ancients Mercury, the god of commerce, was also the god of thieves. This is true, that the merchant and the thief are alike in taking account *exclusively* of their own interest to the detriment of those with whom they have to do.

The fact that in our present society production does not take place generally to provide for the needs of men, but for many other reasons, has important effects upon the character of those who possess the means of production. Production is carried on for profit exclusively; if greater profits can be made by stopping production it will be stopped—this is the point of view of the capitalists. The consumers, on the other hand, see in production the means of creating what man has need of. The world likes to be deceived, and does not care to recognize the fact that the producer has only his own profit in view. The latter encourages this notion and poses as a disinterested person. If he reduces the price of his wares, he claims to do it in the interest of the public, and takes care not to admit that it is for the purpose of increasing his own profits. This is the falsity that belongs inevitably to capitalism.

In general this characteristic of capitalism has no importance for the morality of the consumer, who is merely duped, but it is far otherwise with the press, which is almost entirely in the power of the capitalists. The press, which ought to be a guide for the masses, and is so in some few cases, in the main is in the hands of capitalists who use it only as a means of making money. In place of being edited by men who, by their ability and firmness, are capable of enlightening the public, newspapers are carried on by persons who see in their calling only a livelihood, and consider only the proprietor of the sheet. In great part the press is the opposite of what it ought to be; it represents the interests of those who pay for advertisements or for articles; it increases the ignorance and the prejudices of the crowd; in a word, it poisons public opinion.

The capitalist takes advantage of this necessitous condition of the worker and exploits him. We have already indicated that capitalism has this trait in common with the earlier methods of production. Little by little one class of men has become accustomed to think that the others are destined to amass wealth for them and to be subservient to them in every way. Slavery, like the wage system, demoralizes the servant as well as the master. With the master it develops cupidity and the imperious character which sees in a fellow man only a being fit to satisfy his desires. It is true that the capitalist has not the power over the proletarian that the master has over his slave; he has neither the right of service nor the power of life and death, yet it is none the less true that he has another weapon against the proletarian, a weapon whose effect is no less terrible, namely enforced idleness. The fact that the supply of manual labor always greatly exceeds the demand puts this weapon into the hands of every capitalist. It is not only the capitalists who carry on any business that are subjected to this influence, but also all who are salaried in their service.

Capitalism exercises in still a third manner an egoistic influence upon the capitalistic "entrepreneur." Each branch has more producers than are necessary. The interests of the capitalists are, then, opposed not only to those of the men from whom they buy or to whom they sell, but also to those of their fellow producers. It is indeed claimed that competition has the effect simply of making the product better and cheaper, but this is looking at the question from only one point of view. The fact which alone affects criminality is that competition forces the participants, under penalty of succumbing, to be as egoistic as possible. Even the producers who have the means of applying all the technical improvements to perfect their product and make it cheaper, are obliged to have recourse to gross deceits in advertising, etc., in order to injure their competitors. Rejoicing at the evil which befalls another, envy at his good fortune, these forms of egoism are the inevitable consequence of competition.

Following the same classification that we employed in the preceding chapter we come now to that part of the bourgeoisie which, without having any occupation, consumes what has been made by others. Not to feel obliged to contribute to the material well-being of humanity in proportion to one's ability must necessarily have a demoralizing influence. A parasite, one who lives without working, does not feel bound by any moral tie to his fellows, but regards them simply as things, instruments meant to serve and amuse him. Their example is a source of demoralization for those about them, and excites the envy of those who see this easy life without the power of enjoying it themselves, and awakes in them the desire to exchange their painful existence for this "dolce far niente."

THE CONDITION OF THE PROLETARIAT

To be thorough we begin by making mention of one of the consequences of the economic position of the proletariat, of which we have already treated briefly, namely the dependence in which persons of this class find themselves in consequence of their lacking the means of production, a state which has a prejudicial influence upon character. The oppressed resort to means which they would otherwise scorn. As we have seen above, the basis of the social feelings is reciprocity. As soon as this is trodden under foot by the ruling class the social sentiments of the oppressed become weak towards them.

The paid labor of the young has a bad influence in several ways.

First, it forces them, while they are still very young, to think only of their own interests; then, brought into contact with persons who are rough and indifferent to their well-being, they follow these only too quickly, because of their imitative tendencies, in their bad habits, grossness of speech, etc. Finally, the paid labor of the young makes them more or less independent at an age where they have the greatest need of guidance. Even if the statistical proof of the influence of the labor of children and young people upon criminality were totally wanting, no one could deny that influence. Child labor is entirely a capitalistic phenomenon, being found especially in the great manufacturing countries like England and Germany. And then one of the most salient facts of criminality is the amount of juvenile crime, which is so enormous that England, followed by other countries, has established a special system to combat this form of criminality. Certainly this increase of juvenile crime is chiefly due to the influence of bad domestic conditions (wage-labor of married women, etc.), but the labor of the young people themselves also plays its part.

It has rightly been said that work has a strong moral influence. But it is also true that immoderate labor has the contrary effect. It brutalizes a man, makes him incapable of elevated sentiments, kills as Key says (in "das Jahrhundert des Kindes"), the man in the beast, while moderate labor ennobles the beast in the man.

The housing conditions of the proletariat have also a significance as regards criminality, and for the special group of sexual offenses their importance is very great. We shall speak of this more fully when we treat especially of these offenses, and will, for the moment, note simply their general consequences.

The disorder and squalor of the home communicate themselves to the inmates; the lack of room obliges the children to live, during a great part of the day, on the streets, with the result that they are brought into contact with all sorts of demoralizing companions. Finally, the living together of a great number of uneducated persons in one small dwelling is the cause of constant quarrels and fights. The situation of those who are merely night-lodgers is especially unfortunate, as we have already seen.

As has already been said at the beginning of these observations as to the influence of the economic life upon the development of social feelings on the part of the proletariat, the egoistic side of the human character is developed by the fact that the individual is dependent, that he lives in a subordinate position, and that he feels himself poor and deprived of everything. However, in so far as the proletarian sells his labor he is guaranteed against famine, however miserable his condition, and conscious of the utility of his rôle in society, he feels himself, notwithstanding his poverty, a man who, except for his employer, is independent of all men. But if work is not to be found, or if the proletarian, sick and infirm, is not able to work, it goes without saying that the resulting unemployment is very demoralizing. The lack of steady work, the horrors of the penury into which he and his fall, and the long train of evils which result from both, kill the social feelings in a man, for, as we have seen above, these feelings depend upon reciprocity. Let one familiarize himself with the thought of the condition of the man who lives in the greatest poverty, *i.e.* the man who is abandoned by all, and he will understand how egoistic must be the feelings of such.

The proletarian is never sure of his existence: like the sword of Damocles unemployment is constantly hanging over his head.

This uncertainty of existence is one of the reasons which explain why, in relatively prosperous times the workingman often spends his wages as soon as he receives them, for he knows that the economies possible to him are so small that he could never be saved from misery in case of unemployment.

Finally we must speak of ignorance and lack of training on the part of the proletariat, as a factor of criminality. As we know, this question of education is one of those which are most debated in criminal sociology.

The ancient idea that crime is only a consequence of ignorance need not be treated of, for morality and intellect are two distinct parts of the psychic life, even though there exists a certain relation between them.

The first reason why ignorance and the lack of general culture must be ranked among the general factors of crime is this: the person who, in our present society, where the great majority of parents care very little for the education of their children, does not go to school, is deprived of the moral ideas (honesty, etc.) which are taught there, and ordinarily passes his time in idleness and vagabondage.

The second reason which makes ignorance a factor of crime, is that generally an ignorant man is, more than others, a man moved by the impulse of the moment, who allows himself to be governed by his passions, and is induced to commit acts which he would not have committed if his intellectual equipment had been different.

In the third place, it is for the following reasons that ignorance and the lack of training fall within the etiology of crime. The mind of the man whose psychic qualities, whether in the domain of the arts, or of the scientists, have been developed, has become less susceptible to evil ideas. His intellectual condition constitutes thus a bridle which can restrain evil thoughts from realizing themselves; for real art and true science strengthen the social instincts.

Finally ignorance is in still another way a factor in crime. Very often the author of a crime conceives and executes it in so clumsy a fashion and with so little chance of success, that we may be certain that he would not have committed it if he had not been an ignorant person, without knowledge of the forces with which he had to do.

When the Italian school is reproached with making their researches upon prisoners only, and not upon criminals and their free equals, the implication is that it is only the stupid and ignorant criminals that are in prison, while the others, the shrewd and tricky, remain at liberty. There is assuredly much truth in this assertion.

In the preceding pages I have already spoken of the influence exercised by bad material surroundings upon a man's character; I have pointed out the moral consequences of bad housing conditions, and also that he becomes embittered and malicious through lack of the necessaries of life. All this applies to the proletariat in general, but much more strongly still to those who do not succeed, for any reason, in selling their labor, that is the lower proletariat.

If the dwellings of the working-class are bad, those of the lower proletariat are more pitiable still. There are, through sickness or lack of work, periods of dire poverty in the life of almost every worker—for the lower proletariat these periods are without intermission. Its poverty is chronic. And when the poverty makes itself felt for a long time together, the intellectual faculties become blunted to such a point that there remains of the man only the brute, struggling for existence.

Although the material and intellectual poverty of the lower proletariat is much greater than that of the proletariat, the difference between them is only quantitative. In one connection, however, there is also a qualitative difference, and a very important one, namely that the working-man is a useful being without whom society could not exist. However oppressed he may be, he is a man who has a feeling of self-respect. It is different with the member of the lower proletariat. He is not useful, but a detriment. He produces nothing, and tries to live upon what others make; he is merely tolerated. He who has lived long in poverty loses all his feeling of self-respect, and lends himself to anything whatever that will suffice to prolong his existence.

In short, poverty (taken in the sense of absolute want), kills the social sentiments in man, destroys in fact all relations between men. He who is abandoned by all can no longer have any feeling for those who have left him to his fate.

SUMMARY

When we sum up the results that we have obtained it becomes plain that economic conditions occupy a much more important place in the etiology of crime than most authors have given them.

First we have seen that the present economic system and its consequences weaken the social feelings. The basis of the economic system of our day being exchange, the economic interests of men are necessarily found to be in opposition. This is a trait that capitalism has in common with other modes of production. But its principal characteristic is that the means of production are in the hands of a few, and most men are altogether deprived of them. Consequently, persons who do not possess the means of production are forced to sell their labor to those who do, and these, in consequence of their economic preponderance, force them to make the exchange for the mere necessaries of life, and to work as much as their strength permits.

This state of things especially stifles men's social instincts; it develops, on the part of those with power, the spirit of domination, and of insensibility to the ills of others, while it awakens jealousy and servility on the part of those who depend upon them. Further the contrary interests of those who have property, and the idle and luxurious life of some of them, also contribute to the weakening of the social instincts.

The material condition, and consequently the intellectual condition, of the proletariat are also a reason why the moral plane of that class is not high. The work of children brings them into contact with persons to associate with whom is fatal to their morals. Long working hours and monotonous labor brutalize those who are forced into them; bad housing conditions contribute also to debase the moral sense, as do the uncertainty of existence, and finally absolute poverty, the frequent consequence of sickness and unemployment. Ignorance and lack of training of any kind also contribute their quota. Most demoralizing of all is the status of the lower proletariat.

The economic position of woman contributes also to the weakening of the social instincts.

The present organization of the family has great importance as regards criminality. It charges the legitimate parents with the care of the education of the child; the community concerns itself with the matter very little. It follows that a great number of children are brought up by persons who are totally incapable of doing it properly. As regards the children of the proletariat, there can be no question of the education properly so-called, on account of the lack of means and the forced absence of one or both of the parents. The school tends to remedy this state of things, but the results do not go far enough. The harmful consequences of the present organization of the family make themselves felt especially in the case of children of the lower proletariat, orphans, and illegitimate children. For these the community does but little, though their need of adequate help is the greatest.

Prostitution, alcoholism, and militarism, which result, in the last analysis, from the present social order, are phenomena that have demoralizing consequences.

As to the different kinds of crime, the very important group of economic criminality finds its origin on the one side in the absolute poverty and the cupidity brought about by the present economic environment, and on the other in the moral abandonment and bad education of the children of the poorer classes. Then, professional criminals are principally recruited from the class of occasional criminals, who, finding themselves rejected everywhere after their liberation, fall lower and lower. The last group of economic crimes (fraudulent bankruptcy, etc.) is so intimately connected with our present mode of production, that it would not be possible to commit it under another.

The relation between sexual crimes and economic conditions is less direct; nevertheless these also give evidence of the decisive influence of these conditions. We have called attention to the four following points.

First, there is a direct connection between the crime of adultery and the present organization of society, which requires that the legal dissolution of a marriage should be impossible or very difficult.

Second, sexual crimes upon adults are committed especially by unmarried men; and since the number of marriages depends in its turn upon the economic situation, the connection is clear; and those who commit these crimes are further almost exclusively illiterate, coarse, raised in an environment almost without sexual morality, and regard the sexual life from the wholly animal side.

Third, the causes of sexual crime upon children are partly the same as those of which we have been speaking, with the addition of prostitution.

Fourth, alcoholism greatly encourages sexual assaults.

As to the relation between crimes of vengeance and the present constitution of society, we have noted that it produces conflicts without number; statistics have shown that those who commit them are almost without exception poor and uncivilized, and that alcoholism is among the most important causes of these crimes.

Infanticide is caused in part by poverty, and in part by the opprobrium incurred by the unmarried mother (an opprobrium resulting from the social utility of marriage).

Political criminality comes solely from the economic system and its consequences.

Finally, economic and social conditions are also important factors in the etiology of degeneracy, which is in its turn a cause of crime.

Upon the basis of what has gone before, we have a right to say that the part played by economic conditions in criminality is preponderant, even decisive.

This conclusion is of the highest importance for the prevention of crime. If it were principally the consequence of innate human qualities (atavism, for example), the pessimistic conclusion that crime is a phenomenon inseparably bound up with the social life would be well founded. But the facts show that it is rather the optimistic conclusions that we must draw, that where crime is the consequence of economic and social conditions, we can combat it by changing those conditions.

However important crime may be as a social phenomenon, however terrible may be the injuries and the evil that it brings upon humanity, the development of society will not depend upon the question as to what are the conditions which could restrain crime or make it disappear, if possible; the evolution of society will proceed independently of this question.

What is the direction that society will take under these continual modifications? This is not the place to treat fully of this subject. In my opinion the facts indicate quite clearly what the direction will be. The productivity of labor has increased to an unheard of degree, and will assuredly increase in the future. The concentration of the means of production into the hands of a few progresses continually; in many branches it has reached such a degree that the fundamental principle of the present economic system, competition, is excluded, and has been replaced by monopoly. On the other hand the working class is becoming more and more organized, and the opinion is very generally held among working-men that the causes of material and intellectual poverty can be eliminated only by having the means of production held in common.

Supposing that this were actually realized, what would be the consequences as regards criminality? Let us take up this question for a moment. Although we can give only personal opinions as to the details of such a society, the general outlines can be traced with certainty.

The chief difference between a society based upon the community of the means of production and our own is that material poverty would be no longer known. Thus one great part of economic criminality (as also one part of infanticide) would be rendered impossible, and one of the greatest demoralizing forces of our present society would be eliminated. And then, in this way those social phenomena so productive of crime, prostitution and alcoholism, would lose one of their principal factors. Child labor and overdriving would no longer take place, and bad housing, the source of much physical and moral evil, would no longer exist.

With material poverty there would disappear also that intellectual poverty which weighs so heavily upon the proletariat; culture would no longer be the privilege of some, but a possession common to all. The consequences of this upon criminality would be very important, for we have seen that even in our present society with its numerous conflicts, the members of the propertied classes, who have often but a veneer of civilization, are almost never guilty of crimes of vengeance. There is the more reason to admit that in a society where interests were not opposed, and where civilization was universal, these crimes would be no longer present, especially since alcoholism also proceeds in large part from the intellectual poverty of the poorer classes. And what is true of crimes of vengeance, is equally true of sexual crimes in so far as they have the same etiology.

A large part of the economic criminality (and also prostitution to a certain extent) has its origin in the cupidity excited by the present economic environment. In a society based upon the community of the means of production, great contrasts of fortune would, like commercial capital, be lacking, and thus cupidity would find no food. These crimes will not totally disappear so long as there has not been a redistribution of property according to the maxim, "to each according to his needs," something that will probably be realized, but not in the immediate future.

The changes in the position of woman which are taking place in our present society, will lead, under this future mode of production, to her economic independence, and consequently to her social independence as well. It is accordingly probable that the criminality of woman will increase in comparison with that of man during the transition period. But the final result will be the disappearance of the harmful effects of the economic and social preponderance of man.

As to the education of children under these new conditions it is difficult to be definite. However, it is certain that the community will concern itself seriously with their welfare. It will see to it that the children whose parents cannot or will not be responsible for them, are well cared for. By acting in this way it will remove one of the most important causes of crime. There is no doubt that the community will exercise also a strict control over the education of children; it cannot be affirmed, however, that the time will come when the children of a number of parents will be brought up together by capable persons; this will depend principally upon the intensity that the social sentiments may attain.

As soon as the interests of all are no longer opposed to each other, as they are in our present society, there will no longer be a question either of politics ("a fortiori" of political *crimes*) or of militarism.

Such a society will not only remove the causes which now make men egoistic, but will awaken, on the contrary, a strong feeling of altruism. We have seen that this was already the case with the primitive peoples, where their economic interests were not in opposition. In a larger measure this will be realized under a mode of production in common, the interests of all being the same.

In such a society there can be no question of crime properly so called. The eminent criminologist, Manouvrier, in treating of the prevention of crime expresses himself thus: "The maxim to apply is, act so that every man shall always have more interest in being useful to his fellows than in harming them." It is precisely in a society where the community of the means of production has been realized that this maxim will obtain its complete application. There will be crimes committed by pathological individuals, but this will come rather within the sphere of the physician than that of the judge. And then we may even reach a state where these cases will decrease in large measure, since the social causes of degeneracy will disappear, and procreation by degenerates be checked through the increased knowledge of the laws of heredity and the increasing sense of moral responsibility.

"It is society that prepares the crime," says the true adage of Quetelet. For all those who have reached this conclusion, and are not insensible to the sufferings of humanity, this statement is sad, but contains a ground of hope. It is sad, because society punishes severely those who commit the crime which she has herself prepared. It contains a ground of hope, since it promises to humanity the possibility of some day delivering itself from one of its most terrible scourges.

HEALY, SELLIN & SUTHERLAND: EARLY TWENTIETH CENTURY AMERICAN CRIMINOLOGY

America in the first part of the twentieth century was a veritable cornucopia of research in social science. The studies done in the University of Chicago, especially by such people as Clifford Shaw and Frederic Thrasher, were notable for establishing a strong empirical base for criminal studies in the United States and in reinstituting an ecological approach to crime from the rather more limited examples of Quetelet and Guerry. The very nature of such studies, however, makes it impossible adequately to represent them by anything less than an extensive quotation. Consequently, I have chosen to conclude with three more concise theoretical statements which I trust are equally representative of American criminology.

Perhaps one of the most sophisticated examples of clinical criminology of this period was the work of William Healy. A physician who founded the Institute for Juvenile Research in the Chicago Juvenile Court, Healy was also director of the Judge Baker Guidance Center in Boston from 1917 to 1947. His diagnostic efforts, though centered at the level of the individual, were far more eclectic than early biotypical theories and increasingly demonstrated Healy's commitment to psychoanalytic theory. The selection here is from the introductory portion of his book The Individual Delinquent.

One of the earlier extensive statements of a conflict theory of crime is by Thorsten Sellin. For many years Professor of Sociology at the University of Pennsylvania and widely acknowledged as one of America's outstanding criminologists, Sellin has produced a multitude of important works in the field. It is only our limited historical interest which confines attention here to his Culture Conflict and Crime.

A final example, without which any discussion of early twentieth century criminology would be incomplete, is Edwin Sutherland's theory of "differential association." Sutherland's work in criminology began in 1921 when theories of crime causation still centered about the controversy between inherited versus acquired factors. In 1924, Sutherland published the first edition of his textbook Criminology in which he was strongly critical of existing criminological theory. In 1939, the third edition of that text contained the first expression of his own theory.

Among other things, this theory fulfilled two requisites in regard to Sutherland's own research. Through several years' association with a career thief who explained how theft is learned much as any other occupation, Sutherland became convinced that criminal behavior might more adequately be explained in terms of cultural factors within the effective milieu of the offender than in terms of some individualistic factor. In addition, Sutherland's growing interest in what he later came to call "white collar crime" made necessary a theory which explained criminality in the upper and middle classes as well as in the lower classes.

The statement of "differential association" here is from the 1939 edition of Principles of Criminology. *This statement of the theory limited its referent to "systematic criminal behavior," a limitation the lack of which in subsequent editions was to play havoc with efforts at empirical testing.*

WILLIAM HEALY

The Individual Delinquent

THE INDIVIDUAL

Dynamic Center of the Problem. The dynamic center of the whole problem of delinquency and crime will ever be the individual offender.

Definite and Practical Knowledge of the Individual is Necessary. It is impossible to get away from the fact that no general theories of crime, sociological, psychological or biological, however well founded, are of much service when the concrete issue, namely the particular offense and the individual delinquent, is before those who have practically to deal with it. The understanding needed is just that craved by Solomon—the understanding of the one who has actually to deal with people, the one who formally is the therapeutist. It does not require prolonged observation of any treatment of the offender to realize what knowledge will prove of most worth in the procedure; one quickly perceives that it must be information concerning characteristic variations of physical and psychical equipment, concerning laws of mental mechanics, and the influence of the various forms of experience on various types of mankind. From this arises scientific and common-sense appreciation of the relation of antecedent to consequent in the life history of the individual offender whose actions and person are to be dealt with.

Collected statistics and groups of facts concerning criminality are offered from time to time as the bases upon which measures of public policy may be erected. So far, however, there has been astonishingly little written into social ordinances as the result of much labor expended in the effort to determine the general facts of crime. There may be several reasons for this. Sometimes the criminologist, even of wide renown, has allowed himself to become almost obsessed by theories and doctrines which have led for the most part only to controversy. But perhaps the greatest cause for slight effect upon legislation and other practical procedure may be found in the fact that when face to face with the complications of the actual case many of the generalizations of criminology are seen to crumble away.

Weakness of General Causation Theories. Nothing is shown by our data more convincingly than the predictable inadequacy of social measures built upon statistics and theories which neglect the fundamental fact of the complexity of causation, determinable through study of the individual case. Many of the works on social misconduct deal with what is often denominated 'general causation,' and attempt to establish geographical, climatological, economic and many other correlations. Much of this is interesting and even seductive, intellectually, and it is true that there are some relationships, such as that between alcoholism and crime, well enough verified to justify social alteration. But that many of these suggested correlations contain only half-truths, one is constrained to believe after prolonged attempt to gather in all available facts in many individual cases. To illustrate a couple of these 'general causation' inferences, we might take the failure of the treatment of drunkards during the last decade under the English Inebriate Acts. It was soon found that the projected curative measures, proposed without any adequate estimation of the personal equipment of those who would come under treatment, could not combat, for example, innate mental deficiencies. In other words, many of the great army of topers are such because of their feeblemindedness, and it is that, and not the ingestion of alcohol, which must be fundamentally reckoned with. For another illustration, we may take the findings, often alluded to, that several forms of crime are more prevalent in certain seasons of the year. Sex assault and violence are notably more frequent during hot weather; is it then safe to assert summer temperature as the main cause? One might well ask, is there not rather a lowering of moral inhibitions during that season through the excess of alcoholic beverages then ingested? The above are two of the very simplest instances of the neglect to ascertain the complexities in the causation of crime. Studies of individual cases, and final summary analysis of these cases, such as we present in the latter part of this work, form the only way of arriving at the truth. Results of such work make the investigator exceedingly chary of theories built upon the consideration of single causes.

Thorough Study Means Balancing of Factors. Thorough study of individual cases does not imply that we shall always find the main cause of the offender's tendency in his own make-up—it merely implies the logical balancing of causative factors. One has seen an extensive family chart exhibited as proof that criminalism is inherited, because of its springing up in several side lines. But in addition to the chart the investigator possessed information that the various persons showing delinquent tendencies all lived in an atrocious environment. The facts not plotted on the chart could be used to show, if we took them also by themselves, that in this family criminalism was uniformly the result of bad social circumstances. On the other hand, it may be conditions in the home, or other environmental agents, which at first sight loom large. But then one finds other individuals in the same family turning out well, others on the same street or with the same associates who do not become criminals. Complicating the argument again, we may discover grave delinquent tendencies appearing in some one member of the most upright families, while, contrariwise, we have occasionally found all the numerous immediate descendants of a terrible drunkard successfully arising in full strength of character from the squalor in which he placed them. So it goes; to single out and blame this or that specific condition, without proceeding by the scientific process of elimination and attempting to rule out other possible causes, will not lead far towards real solutions. Indeed, without well-rounded studies of the pivotal facts in the particular case it ensues that "experience is fallacious and judgment difficult."

Growth of Idea of Studying the Offender. The idea that the individual must be carefully studied in order that crime may be ameliorated has been steadily growing since the day of Lombroso. The humanitarian efforts of John Howard were evidence of the appreciation of the needs of offenders as individual human beings; the view of Lombroso was that of the scientific man who sees in this field the inexorable laws which govern man's nature and environment. It makes little difference which theoretical view of penology is held; the problem of society ever is to handle a given offender satisfactorily. Recently the Japanese authority, Oba, a strong believer in the necessity of meeting evil by evil, maintains that at the beginning of the handling of the offender there must be the most exact research into the characteristics and conditions of both him and his family. In his plans for effectively dealing with recidivism this writer insists that only through such a method could the punishment be made proportionate to the guilt—and that is a prime necessity in his scheme.

The Problem of Personality. Clear comprehension of the make-up of human personality will prove a gain to the student of our subject. A person is not fairly to be regarded merely as the soul and body of the moment. It is only our own temporal limitations which prevent us from seeing people as they really are—as products of the loom of time. Every individual is partly his ancestors, and partly the result of his developmental conditions, and partly the effects of many reactions to environment, and to bodily experiences, and even of reactions to his own mental activities. An ideal description of a human person would refer each trait or condition to its proper source. Most serviceable to us is the conception of the individual as the product of conditions and forces which have been actively forming him from the earliest moment of his unicellular life. To know him completely would be to know accurately these conditions and forces; to know him as well as is possible, all of his genetic background that is ascertainable should be known. The interpretations that may be derived from acquaintance with the facts of ancestry, ante-natal life, childhood development, illnesses and injuries, social experiences, and the vast field of mental life, lead to invaluable understandings of the individual and to some idea of that wonderful complex of results which we term personality.

THE MENTAL BASES OF DELINQUENCY

Conduct an Expression of Mental Life. All conduct is directly an expression of mental life. Immediately back of the action is the idea, or the wish, or the impulse, existing as mental content. Of course many actions have no representation in consciousness, either before or after performance, but nevertheless they are just as truly controlled by mental processes. One starts to walk down the street, thereby engaging in public conduct, and continues to walk, and finally stops; all without the slightest thought about this succession of acts. Yet every part of the performance has been impelled by operations of the mind, that part of the mind which, fortunately for our ability to pay attention to other things, is subconscious. Proof of all this is found in the normal power to produce similar action as consciously controlled behavior; to see, as it were, how it was done. More evidence on the same point is derived from our ready recollection that actions arose from mental activity which at the moment of action was not above the threshold of consciousness. We remember how we walked down the street and that the walking was carried out at the bidding of our desires, although we did not at the time formulate this sequence. Altogether, a great deal of mental life at any given moment is subconscious, and a great deal of conduct which appears for the moment uncontrolled, nevertheless is directly dependent on subconscious mental activity.

Even conduct in the pathological mental states which supervene during the varied conditions of epilepsy or insanity is just as truly the direct outcome of mental activity, although not controlled by the conscious will, and frequently not in the least representable at any time in consciousness. The anti-social actions of such periods are the fault of the disordered mental mechanism which at the time precludes normal conscious mental life. Disordered though the higher mentality may then be, some parts of the mind are actively at work creating conduct. We can be sure of this through the easy determination of hallucinations and morbid ideations and impulsions which are often discernible in such cases.

In its physiological aspect conduct may be traced back to origins which, reasoning from the well-established correlation of brain-cell activity with mental life, show also the mental processes back of the deed. Conduct may be readily stated in terms of muscular action; the latter activity, in turn, is propagated by currents of nervous force which, for all such complicated processes, are known to arise from the coördinated energy of cerebral cells. The parts of the brain involved are the higher levels, those which we know are correlated with mental phenomena rising on occasion above the threshold of consciousness. So it seems that all analysis of the dynamics back of conduct leads directly to contemplation of mental activity.

Practical Bearings of the Psychological Viewpoint. However, for the pragmatic ends of this work, one would not be satisfied with any *a priori* considerations alone, however logically fundamental, in the study of the causative factors of delinquency. To be suited for our purposes, such a line of approach as the above must present tangible evidences of practical worth. It must appear that by deliberately turning our studies towards the phenomena of mental life, paths will be discovered to amendment of the moral situation. The psychological point of view, if it fail in this, must be discarded as not inherently essential.

In taking up the actual problem of the sources of delinquency it was apparent that just this method of approach afforded the quickest and clearest understanding, the surest interpretation, and by far the greatest promise of success; and altogether was a much less difficult path to follow than might be expected. Our own case studies have generally led us to the overwhelming conclusion that, for practical purposes, what we particularly want to know about the offender are the immediate mental antecedents of his conduct.

Misconduct is only a branch of conduct in general; and nowhere can the relationships between conduct and mental life be perceived better than in studying the immediate causations of social misdoing. The robbery was preceded by the mental presentation, the plan; the assault followed upon the mental reaction of anger to the displeasing pictures which the spoken word brought up; the temptation was followed because the idea of immediate satisfaction was not counterbalanced just then by conscious representation of consequences. Thus illustrations might be indefinitely multiplied of how a mental process immediately precedes conduct.

Hence it is clear *whatever* influences the individual towards offense must influence first the mind of the individual. It is only because the bad companion puts dynamically significant pictures into the mind, or because the physical activity becomes a sensation with representation in psychic life, or the environmental conditions produce low mental perceptions of one's duty towards others, that there is any inclination at all towards delinquency.

So true is this that, through application of the methods of individual study, it soon becomes apparent that really the only safe way to ascertain the driving forces which make for social offense is to get at the mental mechanisms antecedent to the behavior in question.

Not reckoning with the mental factor leads to many errors in the drawing of conclusions. The force of the actual findings is the strongest argument against the student of delinquency becoming an externalist, an investigator merely of outward and overt circumstances. If the facts are taken all together the following sorts of complications are to be found: The family life may have been faulty, but it was actually the influence of certain pernicious experiences which made recurrent imagery that has consciously or subconsciously driven to offense. Study of heredity may show wanderers in a family line, but in this member of the family it was a hidden mental conflict about a terrible secret that led to the running away from home. We came to know this because we brought the conflict to light, and the light cured both it and the running away. In another case frightful crowding of the home could not be blamed except that it induced ideas and mental pictures which led straight to bad conduct.

Such facts, and what is brought about by differential psychology, give some suggestion as to why other persons in the same family, or house, or street, or gang, have not turned to delinquency. These comparisons should be ever a barrier to the acceptance of general social or biological theories of crime. Realization of the mental factors must prevent our giving credit to mouth-filling declarations that crime is an atavistic phenomenon, or a disease, or that "the criminal" belongs to this or that human sub-species—declarations in which definition is bought for too cheap an intellectual outlay.

Importance of Mental Abnormality. Turning now to abnormal mental traits and conditions correlated with delinquency, we have further corroboration of mental life standing to conduct as antecedent to consequent. The part insanity plays in the production of social disturbance is too obvious to need illustration. Border-line individuals with their morbid, overwhelming impulsions and compulsions are also well recognized as having a mental equipment prone to develop delinquency. Showing mostly negative aspects we have the mental defectives. In them it is not so much that their actual concepts give rise to delinquency, as that through their lack of judgment and counterbalancing power, influences and suggestions coming either from their own physical selves or from the external world, lead to impulses and pictures which determine the misdeed.

Therefore, even in these abnormal individuals it is clearly improbable that peculiar palates, or insensitive finger tips, or queerly-shaped heads will ever be found in any such close relationship to delinquency as are the mental phenomena we discuss. With full respect for those who earliest apprehended the problem of the delinquent as an individual, we nevertheless see the utter inadequacy of work which did not, first and foremost, determine the offender's mental content, his mental traits, peculiarities and abilities. Vastly important though social and biological backgrounds are, yet they must take at least second place to these more immediate causative factors of delinquency.

We have previously insisted on the impossibility of applying in all cases the criterion of responsibility as definable in the law. We believe this matters little because cases can be satisfactorily handled from other standpoints. But as students of mental life we are forced to unequivocally commit ourselves to the opinion that many individuals who commit misdeeds have abnormal impulsions, or are temporarily or chronically weak in the powers of self-control. This is the basis for the idea of lessened moral responsibility which accords truly with the facts. We may call the attention of the reader to our studies of types primarily defective in self-control, types of those affected by adolescent impulsions, of those assailed by the curious phenomena of the epilepsies, of menstrual mental disorders, of senile failures of inhibition, and so on. When one has surveyed such groups as these, two practical conclusions must be drawn; one, that there often is prodigious difficulty in defining legal responsibility, and, next, that these cases, for their own welfare and for the protection of society, need appropriate physical, educational, or even disciplinary treatment under highly individualized surveillance.

Psychological Standpoint Taken Alone is Unsafe. We will not attempt to review the opinions of the several criminologists who upon *a priori* grounds have already declared themselves for the psychological point of view. We can do better by presenting the facts gleaned from life studies which lead us directly to the same position. The concrete argument is to be read in almost every page of our case histories. Mental and moral problems may there be seen to merge.

Notwithstanding all this I fully recognize that there are many cases in which sole dependence on the psychological standpoint would be a grave mistake. Repeatedly I have asserted the opinion, still held, that it is very difficult to decide which is in general the most important investigatory vantage ground—social, medical, or psychological. The point is clear, however, that one can most surely and safely arrive at remedial measures through investigation of the mental factors.

There is no doubt that certain groups of physicians and educators will best understand the importance of the above truths—physicians who have been especially engaged with psychiatric and neurological problems, and educators who are interested in applied psychology. Sociologists and psychologists have nowadays rapidly growing conceptions of the value of individual study. Those who under the law have to deal with offenders are, however, foremost in needing to understand fundamentals. And if it be intimated that these issues are too abstruse, we should feel justified in asserting that those who have not the capacity to appreciate these things are certainly not fitted to pass judgments on delinquents or hold authority over them.

Specific Features of Mental Life Underlying Delinquency. This chapter, dealing with the general survey of the mental bases of delinquency, is hardly the proper place in which to offer specific details. Not that the fundamentals are too technical, but that they are best presented in connection with concrete findings. The study of actual cases is imperative for understanding the part which mental life plays in the production of misconduct. It may be useful here, however, to itemize some of those features of mental life which study shows directly underlie delinquency. Perusal of concrete instances in the second part of this volume will lead to completer understanding of what is now merely enumerated. The proof of the validity of the psychological data will often be found in the actual outcome of the case as predicted in accordance with them.

We may find existing as bases of delinquency any of the following:

Mental dissatisfactions; those developed from cravings of no special moral significance in themselves, or even from unfulfilled creditable ambitions.

Criminalistic imagery, sometimes fairly obsessional, which persists, and is strong enough to impel misconduct.

Irritative mental reactions to environmental conditions, seeking expression or relief in misdoing.

The development of habits of thought involving persistent criminalistic ideas and reactions.

Adolescent mental instabilities and impulsions.

Mental conflicts, worries or repressions concerning various experiences or matters of mental content. These sometimes interfere with that smooth working of the inner life which fosters socially normal conduct. The misdeed here, too, may be a relief phenomenon.

The chronic attitude of the offender representing himself to himself as one, like Ishmael, whose hand shall be against every man and every man's hand against him. The remarkable phenomenon of anti-social grudge may be included here.

Mental peculiarities or twists which are agents in the production of anti-social conduct, but which do not overwhelm the personality enough to warrant us in grading the subject as aberrational.

Aberrational mental states:—all the way from fully-developed psychoses to temporary or border-line psychotic conditions.

Mental defect in any of the several forms described in our special chapter on the subject.

THORSTEN SELLIN

Culture Conflict and Crime

THE NATURE OF CONDUCT NORMS

Man is born into a culture. He arrives biologically equipped to receive and to adapt knowledge about himself and his relationships to others. His first social contacts begin a life-long process of coordination during which he absorbs and adapts ideas which are transmitted to him formally or informally by instruction or precept. These ideas embody *meanings* attached to customs, beliefs, artifacts, and his own relationships to his fellow men and to social institutions. Looked upon as discreet units, these ideas may be regarded as *cultural elements*, which fit into patterns or configurations of ideas, which tend to become fixed into integrated systems of meanings. Embodied in the mind they become *personality elements,* and the sum total of all such elements may be conveniently called *personality,* as distinguished from the person's biological individuality or his inherited and acquired morphological and physiological traits. Personality then rests upon a biological foundation, which is of the greatest importance in the formation of personality. The biological make-up of an individual fixes limits to personality development, determines the character of the receptive and adaptive processes which transform cultural elements into personality elements, and influences the latter's expressions in social activity.

This definition of personality is not acceptable to all sociologists, not to mention the representatives of other disciplines. In a recent work Gordon W. Allport analyzes no fewer than forty-eight definitions and then proposes one of his own. The one adopted above and previously used by W. I. Thomas, Ellsworth Faris, and others, he criticizes as being the result of a failure to realize that "personality is more than 'the subjective side of culture'—a truth that sociologists and cultural anthropologists with their one-sided studies of 'culture and personality' are likely to forget." This critique assumes that psychologists *know* what personality is, when all that can be said is that for the purpose of psychological research, any sociological definition of personality is inadequate. For the same reason, sociologists insist on defining their own terms of inquiry. In studying social phenomena, they are compelled to pay attention to the person, but they see him primarily as the focus of group influences, a product of social conditioning, a social microcosm. If they prefer to use the term personality as the label for the "subjective aspect of culture," they may be criticized for contributing to the confusion of language by employing a term which is used in so many different senses that it makes rigid thinking difficult, but they can not be criticized for placing upon their inquiries the limitations imposed by their science. This does not mean that the sociologist is not interested in "the dynamic organization within the individual of those psychophysical systems that determine his unique adjustment to his environment" and that these "psycho-physical systems" can be left out of consideration in the study of social phenomena. It does mean, however, that sociologists are not prepared to investigate these "systems," since they are not psychologists or biologists; and that they have to rely on those scientists to define them. The value of such definitions to the sociologist can then be tested by him in his own way.

If all individuals were biologically alike and subjected to identical cultural influences, all personalities would be identical. If all individuals were biologically alike, but each subjected to different cultural influences, each would present unique personality configurations. Since with the possible exceptions of identical twins, no two individuals can be found that possess the same biological equipment and since no two persons can ever be assumed to have been exposed to the same cultural influences, at least after the period of early infancy, each total personality is unique. Scientific research in the behavior field is therefore confronted with the problem of offering scientific descriptions of the growth and manifestations of unique personalities in unique biological individuals. The scientific method, however, is not applicable to the study of unique phenomena. It can only deal with classes, kinds, types. If a generalization were made on the basis of the findings in a study of a case assumed to be unique, the validity of that generalization could never be tested. Etiological research would be impossible if it could not assume that the data it employs may be grouped into classes, the units of which are identical or may at least be assumed to possess sufficient similarity to be classed together for research purposes.

Every person's existence may be regarded from one point of view at least as being made up of one choice after another. He is constantly faced with the need of deciding whether he should do this or do that. The vast majority of these choices are of an undramatic nature, involving the prosaic routine of daily life and so affected by habit that the deliberative element associated with the idea of "choice" has been submerged and the person's reaction has gradually become automatic. Such being the case, it is the new or the infrequently recurring situation in which he finds himself which most obviously calls into action the exercise of the will and compels him to balance against one another the various possible reactions which the life situation in question arouses, selecting the one he deems most suitable to him at the moment. Whether the manner in which a person responds in a situation is the result of habit or of deliberation, his reaction may be regarded as an expression of his personality. The character of that reaction depends upon what the life situation involved *means* to him. Some of these life situations, at least are sufficiently repetitious and socially so defined that they call for definite responses from the type of person who encounters them. There are attached to them, so to speak, norms which define the reaction of response which in a given person is approved or disapproved by the normative group. The social attitude of this group toward the various ways in which a person might act under certain circumstances has thus been crystallized into a rule, the violation of which arouses a group reaction. These rules or norms may be called *conduct norms*. All personal reaction or activity which they govern may be called *conduct*. The term behavior might well be reserved for all types of reactions—conduct then being a subtype—or for all types *not* defined as conduct.

Conduct, as defined above, can occur only in situations which are defined by some social group and governed by a rule of some sort. Furthermore, all conduct has been socially conditioned, since personality is a social product. Therefore, it is unwise from a scientific point of view to speak of antisocial as opposed to social conduct. These terms belong to the language of social reform. It would seem best, in order to avoid misunderstanding, to speak instead of *normal* and *abnormal conduct,* i.e. conduct in accord with or deviating from a conduct norm.

Conduct norms are the products of social life. Social groups place on the activity of their members certain restrictions which aim to insure the protection of social values which have been injured by unrestricted conduct. A conduct norm is originally an *ex post facto* rule. Generally speaking "breach is the mother of law" and equally a mother of conduct norms.

Every person is identified with a number of social groups, each meeting some biologically conditioned or socially created need. Each of these groups is normative in the sense that within it there grow up norms of conduct applicable to situations created by that group's specific activities. As a member of a given group, a person is not only supposed to conform to the rules which it shares with other groups, but also to those which are peculiarly its own. A person who as a member of a family group—in turn the transmitting agency for the norms which governed the groups from which the parents came—possesses all its norms pertaining to conduct in routine life situations, may also as a member of a play group, a work group, a political group, a religious groups, etc., acquire norms which regulate specialized life situations and which sustain, weaken or even contradict the norms earlier incorporated in his personality. The more complex a culture becomes, the more likely it is that the number of normative groups which affect a person will be large, and the greater is the chance that the norms of these groups will fail to agree, no matter how much they may overlap as a result of a common acceptance of certain norms. A conflict of norms is said to exist when more or less divergent rules of conduct govern the specific life situation in which a person may find himself. The conduct norm of one group of which he is a part may permit one response to this situation, the norm of another group may permit perhaps the very opposite response.

For every person, then, there is from the point of view of a given group of which he is a member, a normal (right) and an abnormal (wrong) way of reacting, the norm depending upon the social values of the group which formulated it. *Conduct norms are, therefore, found wherever social groups are found, i.e. universally. They are not the creation of any* ONE *normative group; they are not confined within political boundaries; they are not necessarily embodied in law.*

These facts lead to the inescapable conclusion that the study of conduct norms would afford a sounder basis for the development of scientific categories than a study of crimes as defined in the criminal law. Such study would involve the isolation and classification of norms into *universal categories,* transcending political and other boundaries, a necessity imposed by the logic of science. The study of how conduct norms develop, how they are related to each other and to other cultural elements, the study of changes and differentials in norm violations and the relationship of such violations to other cultural phenomena, are certainly questions which the sociologist by training and interest might regard as falling within his field. They are questions which scholars such as Lévy-Bruhl and Bayet would include within the framework of what the latter calls *ethology*—not to be confused with John Stuart Mill's characterology to which he gave the same label—or the discipline which attempts to formulate the scientific generalizations governing the structure, growth, and relationships of "moral facts"!

The need for finding some basis for criminological research which would extend beyond that of the law has been expressed before. Innumerable definitions of crime have been offered which if not read in their context would appear to go beyond the legal definition. Upon examination, however, almost all of them prove to be the legal norms clothed in a sociological language. Such is not the case, however, with the definition offered by Makarewicz, who can be said to use the term crime in the sense of a conduct norm. "A crime is an act by a member of a given social group, which by the rest of the members of that group is regarded as so injurious or as showing such a degree of antisocial attitude in the actor that the group publicly, overtly and collectively reacts by trying to abrogate someone of his rights *(Güter)*." Znaniecki also attempts to avoid the legal definition and in his latest work we find the following statement which presents his point of view. "Because a collective system has social validity in the eyes of each and all of those who share in it, because it is endowed with a special dignity which merely individual systems lack altogether, individual behavior which endangers a collective system and threatens to harm any of its elements appears quite different from an agression against an individual (unless, of course, such an agression hurts collective values as well as individual values). It is not only a harmful act, but an objectively evil act, a violation of social validity, an offense against the superior dignity of this collective system. . . . The best term to express the specific significance of such behavior is *crime*. We are aware that in using the word in this sense, we are giving it a much wider significance than it has in criminology. *But we believe, that it is desirable for criminology to put its investigations on a broader basis; for strictly speaking, it still lacks a proper theoretic basis.* . . . Legal qualifications are not founded on the results of previous research and not made for the purpose of future research; therefore they have no claim to be valid as scientific generalizations—nor even as heuristic hypotheses." This extension of the meaning of the term *crime* is not desirable. It is wiser to retain that term for the offenses made punishable by the criminal law and to use the term abnormal conduct for the violations of norms whether legal or not.

THE CONFLICT OF CONDUCT NORMS

In the second chapter of this monograph an attempt has been made to provide a frame of reference for sociological research on abnormal conduct, of which crime is but one form distinguished from others by the fact that it violates the conduct norms specifically defined by the criminal law. If the analysis there presented is sound, the conclusions must be that the study of legal norms, their violations and violators should be conceived in ethological instead of legal terms. These conclusions may be regarded by some persons as unfounded, even perhaps as presumptuous or fantastic, but the writer at least is sincerely convinced that the basic problem upon which they rest is a real one and that upon its solution rests the future of scientific research in the criminological field. The barriers which the criminal law has erected about that field must somehow be razed.

Since in recent years a number of studies have been made on "culture conflict" and delinquency, studies which assume the existence of legal and nonlegal conduct norms in conflict with each other, it is natural to suppose that an examination of some of these researches and their theoretical framework may afford the opportunity to make a breach in the barriers to which reference has been made. The examination completed, some suggestions concerning further studies may be appropriate. .

As is natural in a nascent science like sociology, the concept of culture conflict has not yet been clearly formulated. The phenomena which the term denotes are not viewed in the same manner by all scholars. They are sometimes regarded as by-products of a cultural growth process—the growth of civilization—sometimes as the result of the migration of conduct norms from one culture complex or area to another. However produced, they are sometimes studied as mental conflicts and sometimes as the clash of cultural codes.

In a recent article, Frank Speck characterized the Labrador Indians in the following words: "The Montagnais-Naskapi of the Labrador peninsula illustrate for us, as well as any contemporary human group could, I fancy, an example of the intimate face-to-face type of society which is so often sought for by the social theorists. We have some of these types of cooperative primitive society in Australia, South Africa and South America. They are primary in pattern, since, through the intimate association of individuals forming them, the social fusion of kin results in producing a community whole within which there is a tendency toward harmony and the most thorogoing cooperation. Strife is scarcely present, violence strenuously avoided; competition even courteously disdained. These, they think, lead to ridicule. In their place are met subjection of self, generosity in respect to property, service and opinion, the qualities which we often speak of as being found in 'good sports' and which seem to develop as social habits. And these are the qualities that to them represent honor and a welcome place in the thoughts of their associates." Of the same group, Lips has more recently spoken, pointing to the "moral heights . . . humanity, and . . . immemorial justice," which "the simple codes of the social life of these Indians show." Here is a group with harmonious, well integrated, consistent cultural norms. The problems of life are solved by means regulated by custom known to all. Of the same character were the self-contained, small and culturally isolated village communities which were the cradle of our Western culture, and which still exist in less rigid or pure form in isolated rural communities of the present day.

From these primitive groups there is a far cry to the modern industrial and mercantile society with its metropolitan aggregations, epitomizing our civilization. The transition, according to the sociologist, was produced by numerous factors, among which inventions, improved means of communication, the growth of population, the interpenetration of cultures, etc., are inextricably mingled and related. Whatever the processes were which resulted in or accompanied this growth, their end product is a culture which instead of the well-knit social fabric, which Speck pictured, shows a multitude of social groups, competitive interests, poorly defined interpersonal relationships, social anonymity, a confusion of norms and a vast extension of impersonal control agencies designed to enforce rules which increasingly lack the moral force which rules receive only when they grow out of emotionally felt community needs. To a large number of persons who live in such a culture, certain life situations are governed by such conflicting norms that no matter what the response of the person in such a situation will be, it will violate the norms of some social group concerned.

To sociologists this picture of modern Western culture suggests maladjustment or disorganization and among its many fruits they find crime, just as the psychiatrist finds neuroses. "The demands of civilized life on man," says a contemporary psychiatrist, "are subtly and cruelly exacting; the fine discriminations demanded of him are innumerable and difficult. He must, first of all, love his parents. Both his natural inclinations and public opinion oblige him to do this. Yet he must emancipate himself from his parents, very often without any encouragement from them; on the contrary, they are rather apt to cling to him emotionally. . . . Furthermore, the child, as he grows up, must inhibit his natural tendencies to acquire the things he wants by direct action; yet he must maintain his capacity and zest for competitive struggle for the goods of this world, in which struggle he must draw a line of hair-like fineness between what is moral and what is immoral or 'wrong.' And although he must acquire property and wealth, if possible, he must also be altruistic, generous, noble. He must be constantly exposed to sex stimulation through visual, aural, and olfactory channels and he must take a manly interest in the other sex in order to be acceptable socially; yet he must remain continent, or find his sexual outlets under . . . conflicting rules, traditions and emotions. . . . He must have strong drives, be aggressive and alert, yet conceal these drives as much as possible. He must have a deep respect for the truth, yet learn to suppress, deny, or distort it on innumerable occasions. On such foundations does our civilization rest. If a man cannot make these fine distinctions he is called a 'rigid personality,' and it seems to be true that such rigid personalities are more liable to mental or emotional derangement." And E. H. Sutherland, contemplating the transformation of our culture from a familistic and cooperative one to an individualistic and competitive one, sees in this process the explanation of crime. The failure of a person "to follow a prescribed pattern of behavior is due to the inconsistency and lack of harmony in the influences which direct the individual. . . . The conflict of cultures is therefore the fundamental principle in the explanation of crime [and] . . . the more the cultural patterns conflict, the more unpredictable is the behavior of the individual." These are the basic hypotheses of his *Principles of Criminology*. They clearly indicate that Sutherland views culture conflict in a manner which makes this "principle" somewhat analogous to, let us say, motion in physics. If all crime is explainable in such a manner, all sociological researches in this field would have to be conceived in terms of culture conflict. This view is not inconsistent with an analysis such as that in chapter II, but it provides merely a framework for research, a way of looking at the task of the sociological criminologist.

It would not be true to say that Professor Sutherland conceives of culture conflicts as arising solely *within* a culture, as a result of the development of disharmonious norms without any introduction of such norms from other cultural areas or systems. Such a condition is, however, with certain reservations, conceivable. The introduction of Western inventions in the Orient has probably given rise within that culture to vastly more conflicts, endogenous in character, than have Western cultural norms transmitted by personal contact or impersonal means of communication, the work of missionaries and traders notwithstanding. Similarly we might defend the thesis, that given the enormous natural resources of the United States and the enterprising character of the early colonists, a culture exhibiting all the "disorganization" to which reference has been made could have developed even without the influx of national and racial groups from cultural or subcultural areas in different parts of the globe, or without contact with other cultures. The conflicts even now pointed to as existing between the norms of negroes and whites in the United States can hardly be regarded as of anything but indigenous origin. There exists no modern culture, however, which has developed without a large amount of borrowing from other cultures, and when we speak therefore of conflicts as arising within a culture as a by-product of a growth process, we are merely stating what seems to be the emphasis which is placed by some scholars on one important aspect of a wider problem. The delinquency area studies of Clifford Shaw, for instance, indicate that in urban areas characterized by great poverty, bad housing, bad neighborhood influences, child gangs, etc., these very conditions give rise to social attitudes which conflict with the norms of the law. While Shaw stresses the fact that these areas are, in the cities he has studied, largely inhabited by European immigrants, this fact would appear to be of minor importance, since he has shown that no matter from what country these immigrants came, the delinquency rates of their children ultimately approach each other after exposure to the conditions mentioned. It is likely that in large European cities with homogeneous populations, the same conditions breed high delinquency.

Conflicts of conduct norms may arise in a different manner from that just described. There are social groups on the surface of the earth which possess complexes of conduct norms which, due to differences in the mode of life and the social values evolved by these groups, appear to set them apart from other groups in many or most respects. We may expect conflicts of norms when the rural dweller moves to the city, but we assume that he has absorbed the basic norms of the culture which comprises both town and country. How much greater is not the conflict likely to be when Orient and Occident meet, or when the Corsican mountaineer is transplanted to the lower East Side of New York. Conflicts of cultures are inevitable when the norms of one cultural or subcultural area migrate to or come in contact with those of another, and it is interesting to note that most of the specific researches on culture conflict and delinquency have been concerned with this aspect of conflict rather than the one mentioned earlier.

Conflicts between the norms of divergent cultural codes may arise

(1) when these codes clash on the border of contiguous culture areas;
(2) when, as may be the case with legal norms, the law of one cultural group is extended to cover the territory of another; or
(3) when members of one cultural group migrate to another.

Speck, for instance, notes that "where the bands popularly known as Montagnais have come more and more into contact with Whites, their reputation has fallen lower among the traders who have known them through commercial relationships within that period. The accusation is made that they have become less honest in connection with their debts, less trustworthy with property, less truthful, and more inclined to alcoholism and sexual freedom as contacts with the frontier towns have become easier for them. Richard White reports in 1933 unusual instances of Naskapi breaking into traders' store houses."

Similar illustrations abound in the works of the cultural anthropologists. We need only to recall the effect on the American Indian of the culture conflicts induced by our policy of acculturation by guile and force. In this instance, it was not merely contact with the white man's culture, his religion, his business methods, and his liquor, which weakened the tribal mores. In addition, the Indian became subject to the white man's law and this brought conflicts as well, as has always been the case when legal norms have been imposed upon a group previously ignorant of them. Maunier, in discussing the diffusion of French law in Algeria, recently stated: "In introducing the *Code Pénal* in our colonies, as we do, we transform into offenses the ancient usages of the inhabitants which their customs permitted or imposed. Thus, among the Khabyles of Algeria, the killing of adulterous wives is ritual murder committed by the father or brother of the wife and not by her husband, as elsewhere. The woman having been sold by her family to her husband's family, the honor of her relatives is soiled by her infidelity. Her father or brother has the right and duty to kill her in order to cleanse by her blood the honor of her relatives. Murder in revenge is also a duty, from family to family, in case of murder of or even in case of insults to a relative; the vendetta, called the *rekba* in Khabylian, is imposed by the law of honor. But these are crimes in French law! Murder for revenge, being premeditated and planned, is assassination, punishable by death! . . . What happens, then, often when our authorities pursue the criminal, guilty of an offense against public safety as well as against morality: public enemy of the French order, but who has acted in accord with a respected custom? The witnesses of the assassination, who are his relatives, or neighbors, fail to lay any charges against the assassin; when they are questioned, they pretend to know nothing; and the pursuit is therefore useless. A French magistrate has been able to speak of 'the conspiracy of silence among Algerians;' a conspiracy aiming to preserve traditions, always followed and obeyed, against their violation by our power. This is the tragic aspect of the conflict of laws. A recent decree forbids the husband among the Khabyles to profit arbitrarily by the power given him according to this law to repudiate his wife, demanding that her new husband pay an exorbitant price for her—this is the custom of the *lefdi*. Earlier, one who married a repudiated wife paid nothing to the former husband. It appears that the first who tried to avail himself of the new law was killed for violating the old custom. The abolition of the ancient law does not always occur without protest or opposition. That which is a crime was a duty; and the order which we cause to reign is sometimes established to the detriment of 'superstition'; it is the gods and the spirits, it is believed, that would punish any one who fails to revenge his honor."

When Soviet law was extended to Siberia, similar effects were observed. Anossow and Wirschubski both relate that women among the Siberian tribes, who in obedience to the law, laid aside their veils were killed by their relatives for violating one of the most sacred norms of their tribes.

The relations between delinquency and the migration of the members of one cultural group to the area of another will be discussed later in this chapter.

We have noted that culture conflicts are the natural outgrowth of processes of social differentiation, which produce an infinity of social groupings, each with its own definitions of life situations, its own interpretations of social relationships, its own ignorance or misunderstandings of the social values of other groups. The transformation of a culture from a homogeneous and well-integrated type to a heterogeneous and disintegrated type is therefore accompanied by an increase of conflict situations. Conversely, the operation of integrating processes will reduce the number of conflict situations. Such conflicts within a changing culture may be distinguished from those created when different cultural systems come in contact with one another, regardless of the character or stage of development of these systems. In either case, the conduct of members of a group involved in the conflict of codes will in some respects be judged abnormal by the other group.

THE STUDY OF CULTURE CONFLICTS

In the study of culture conflicts, some scholars have been concerned with the effect of such conflicts on the conduct of specific persons, an approach which is naturally preferred by psychologists and psychiatrists and by sociologists who have used the life history technique. These scholars view the conflict as internal. Wirth states categorically that a culture "conflict can be said to be a factor in delinquency only if the individual feels it or acts as if it were present." Culture conflict is mental conflict, but the character of this conflict is viewed differently by the various disciplines which use this term. Freudian psychiatrists regard it as a struggle between deeply rooted biological urges which demand expression and the culturally created rules which give rise to inhibitive mechanisms which thwart this expression and drive them below the conscious level of the mind, whence they rise either by ruse in some socially acceptable disguise, as abnormal conduct when the inhibiting mechanism breaks down, or as neuroses when it works too well. The sociologist, on the other hand, thinks of mental conflict as being primarily the clash between antagonistic conduct norms incorporated in personality. "Mental conflict in the person," says Burgess in discussing the case presented by Shaw in *The Jack-Roller*, "may always be explained in terms of the conflict of divergent cultures."

If this view is accepted, sociological research on culture conflict and its relationships to abnormal conduct would have to be strictly limited to a study of the personality of cultural hybrids. Significant studies could be conducted only by the life-history case technique applied to persons in whom the conflict is internalized, appropriate control groups being utilized, of course.

The absence of mental conflict, in the sociological sense, may, however, be well studied in terms of culture conflict. An example may make this clear. A few years ago a Sicilian father in New Jersey killed the sixteen-year-old seducer of his daughter, expressing surprise at his arrest since he had merely defended his family honor in a traditional way. In this case a mental conflict in the sociological sense did not exist. The conflict was external and occurrred between cultural codes or norms. We may assume that where such conflicts occur violations of norms will arise merely because persons who have absorbed the norms of one cultural group or area migrate to another and that such conflict will continue so long as the acculturation process has not been completed. Only then may the violations be regarded in terms of mental conflict.

If culture conflict may be regarded as sometimes personalized, or mental, and sometimes as occurring entirely in an impersonal way solely as a conflict of group codes, it is obvious that research should not be confined to the investigation of mental conflicts and that contrary to Wirth's categorical statement that it is impossible to demonstrate the existence of a culture conflict "objectively . . . by a comparison between two cultural codes" this procedure has not only a definite function, but may be carried out by researches employing techniques which are familiar to the sociologist.

The emphasis on the life history technique has grown out of the assumption that "the experiences of one person at the same time reveals the life activities of his group" and that "habit in the individual is an expression of custom in society." This is undoubtedly one valid approach. Through it we may hope to discover generalizations of a scientific nature by studying persons who (1) have drawn their norms of conduct from a variety of groups with conflicting norms, or (2) who possess norms drawn from a group whose code is in conflict with that of the group which judges the conduct. In the former case alone can we speak of mental or internal culture conflict; in the latter, the conflict is external.

If the conduct norms of a group are, with reference to a given life situation, inconsistent, or if two groups possess inconsistent norms, we may assume that the members of these various groups will individually reflect such group attitudes. Paraphrasing Burgess, the experiences of a group will reveal the life activities of its members. While these norms can, no doubt, be best established by a study of a sufficient number of representative group members, they may for some groups at least be fixed with sufficient certainty to serve research purposes by a study of the social institutions, the administration of justice, the novel, the drama, the press, and other expressions of group attitudes. The identification of the groups in question having been made, it might be possible to determine to what extent such conflicts are reflected in the conduct of their members. Comparative studies based on the violation rates of the members of such groups, the trends of such rates, etc., would dominate this approach to the problem.

In conclusion, then, culture conflict may be studied either as mental conflict or as a conflict of cultural codes. The criminologist will naturally tend to concentrate on such conflicts between legal and nonlegal conduct norms. The concept of conflict fails to give him more than a general framework of reference for research. In practice, it has, however, become nearly synonymous with conflicts between the norms of cultural systems or areas. Most researches which have employed it have been done on immigrant or race groups in the United States, perhaps due to the ease with which such groups may be identified, the existence of more statistical data recognizing such groupings, and the conspicuous differences between some immigrant norms and our norms.

The belief that immigrant groups are largely responsible for our high criminality has been and is frequently expressed. Many have written about the criminality of these groups, but most of their observations have been based on inadequate data. We need only point out that in order to establish the criminality of a group, we must be able to identify this group with a high degree of accuracy and know its size and composition so that proper bases for the computation of rates will be available. Furthermore, we must establish the extent and character of the crimes committed by members of this group, before rates can be computed. In other words, adequate population as well as criminal statistics are necessary. Deficiencies in both these fields of statistics have been responsible for much of the confusion which is evident in the literature, and to these lacks have been added hasty interpretations.

EDWIN SUTHERLAND

Principles of Criminology*

CONSIDERATIONS IN A THEORY OF CRIMINAL BEHAVIOR

Three general considerations should be kept in mind in the construction of a theory of criminology. First, the other theories of criminology should be considered. The various theories of criminology differ principally in the points which they emphasize. These theories may be classified regarding the points of emphasis in two principal groups, namely, individual differences and situational or cultural processes. The individual differences may be inherited or acquired, and may include anatomical and physiological deviations, feeblemindedness, psychopathy, and minor mental and emotional deviations. The situational and cultural processes may place emphasis on small groups such as family and neighborhood, on general institutions such as the economic and political systems, or on general cultural processes such as differential association, cultural conflicts, and social disorganization. All of these must be considered and most of them included in a final organization of thought regarding criminal behavior.

Second, the execution of a crime requires desire for the results to be secured by the crime, lack or weakness of internal inhibitions, lack or weakness of external inhibitions (including accessibility of the object, public opinion or group opinion regarding the behavior, and the danger of detection and punishment), and technical ability to execute the crime. A theory of criminal behavior should take all of these into account. Many of the theories have been concerned only with the desires and inhibitions of the person who commits the crime.

---

* From *Principles of Criminology* by Edwin Sutherland. Reprinted by permission of the publisher, J. B. Lippincott Company. 3rd ed. © 1939.

Third, delinquency is adventitious when considered as a specific act of a specific person. No one can explain why a coin comes up "heads" on a particular toss. It is described as due to chance. Chance does not mean that no causes are operating, but that the causes are so complicated that they cannot be analyzed. Similarly, a specific criminal act may be the result of a complex of causes which cannot be analyzed. This does not mean that it is similar to the flipping of a coin with only two alternatives and those of equal likelihood. Rather it is like rolling loaded dice, with high probability but not certainty. It is not possible to explain adequately why one person commits a specific crime while another, with traits, experiences, and social situation almost identical, does not. The plot of a recent motion picture is based on a comparison of two boys engaged in theft. When discovered, one ran more rapidly, escaped, and became a priest; the other ran less rapidly, was caught and committed to a reformatory, and became a gangster. In other circumstances, the one who ran more rapidly might have become the gangster and the one who ran less rapidly the priest. It is such combinations of factors which make it impossible to explain each individual act adequately, because it is never possible to include all of these unique combinations in a generalization. On that account attention should be concentrated on systematic criminal behavior, either in the form of criminal careers or organized criminal practices. By this statement of the problem it may be possible to discover the processes which are general and uniform and to arrive at an adequate theory of such behavior. If a theory can be developed that is adequate for systematic criminal behavior it will be easier to explain specific acts in relation to this framework.

A THEORY OF CRIMINAL BEHAVIOR

This tentative theory of criminal behavior is stated in the form of the seven following propositions.

First, *the processes which result in systematic criminal behavior are fundamentally the same in form as the processes which result in systematic lawful behavior.* If criminality were specifically determined by inheritance, the laws and principles of inheritance would be the same for criminal behavior and for lawful behavior. The same is true of imitation or any other genetic process in the development of behavior. Criminal behavior differs from lawful behavior in the standards by which it is judged but not in the principles of genetic processes.

Second, *systematic criminal behavior is determined in a process of association with those who commit crimes, just as systematic lawful behavior is determined in a process of association with those who are law-abiding*. Any person can learn any pattern of behavior which he is able to execute. He inevitably assimilates such behavior from the surrounding culture. The pattern of behavior may cause him to suffer death, physical injury, loss of friendship, or loss of money, but it may nevertheless be followed with joy provided he has learned that it is the thing to do. Since criminal behavior is thus developed in association with criminals it means that crime is the cause of crime. In the same manner war is the cause of war, and the Southern practice of dropping the "r" is the cause of the Southern practice of dropping the "r." This proposition, stated negatively, is that a person does not participate in systematic criminal behavior by inheritance. No individual inherits tendencies which inevitably make him criminal or inevitably make him law-abiding. Also, the person who is not already trained in crime does not invent systematic criminal behavior. While personality certainly includes an element of inventiveness, a person does not invent a system of criminal behavior unless he has had training in that kind of behavior, just as a person does not make systematic mechanical inventions unless he has had training in mechanics.

Third, *differential association is the specific causal process in the development of systematic criminal behavior*. The principles of the process of association by which criminal behavior develops are the same as the principles of the process by which lawful behavior develops, but the contents of the patterns presented in association differ. For that reason it is called differential association. The association which is of primary importance in criminal behavior is association with persons who engage in systematic criminal behavior. A person who has never heard of professional shoplifting may meet a professional shoplifter in his hotel, may become acquainted with and like him, learn from him the techniques, values, and codes of shoplifting, and under this tutelage may become a professional shoplifter. He could not become a professional shoplifter by reading newspapers, magazines, or books. The impersonal agencies of communication exert some influence but are important principally in determining receptivity to the patterns of criminal behavior when they are presented in personal association, and in producing incidental offenses. These patterns are presented through the impersonal agencies of communication to everyone in our culture. Every child capable of learning inevitably assimilates knowledge regarding property rights and thefts in the simpler situations. It is probably for this reason that everyone is somewhat criminal. College students, with a few exceptions doubtless due to poor memories, report an average of eight thefts or series of thefts during their lifetimes; a series of thefts in this case may include scores of incidents, such as stealing fruit from neighbors' trees from the age of seven to twelve. These thefts were reported equally for males and females, and continued in most cases to the age at which the reports were made. In the later years they generally took the form of theft of books from the library, of equipment from the gymnasium or laboratory, or of souvenirs from hotels and restaurants. Students do not regard such thefts as especially reprehensible; they regard them as amusing. Similarly, boys in the delinquent areas of cities do not regard thefts of automobiles or the burglary of stores as reprehensible, and business or professional men do not regard their frauds and tricky manipulations as reprehensible. A person engages in those criminal acts which are prevalent in his own groups, and he assimilates them in association with the members of the groups.

Fourth, *the chance that a person will participate in systematic criminal behavior is determined roughly by the frequency and consistency of his contacts with the patterns of criminal behavior.* If a person could come into contact only with lawful behavior he would inevitably be completely law-abiding. If he could come into contact only with criminal behavior (which is impossible, since no group could exist if all of its behavior were criminal) he would inevitably be completely criminal. The actual condition is between these extremes. The ratio of criminal acts to lawful acts by a person is roughly the same as the ratio of the contacts with the criminal and with the lawful behavior of others. It is true, of course, that a single critical experience may be the turning point in a career. But these critical experiences are generally based on a long series of former experiences and they produce their effects generally because they change the person's associations. One of these critical experiences that is most important in determining criminal careers is the first public appearance as a criminal. A boy who is arrested and convicted is thereby publicly defined as a criminal. Thereafter his associations with lawful people are restricted and he is thrown into association with other delinquents. On the other hand a person who is consistently criminal is not defined as law-abiding by a single lawful act. Every person is expected to be law-abiding, and lawful behavior is taken for granted because the lawful culture is dominant, more extensive, and more pervasive than the criminal culture.

Fifth, *individual differences among people in respect to personal characteristics or social situations cause crime only as they affect differential association or frequency and consistency of contacts with criminal patterns.* Poverty in the home may force a family to reside in a low-rent area where delinquency rates are high and thereby facilitate association with delinquents. Parents who insist that their boy return home immediately after school and who are able to enforce this regulation may prevent the boy from coming into frequent contact with delinquents even though the family resides in a high delinquency area. A child who is not wanted at home may be emotionally upset, but the significant thing is that this condition may drive him away from the home and he may therefore come into contact with delinquents. A boy who is timid may be kept from association with rough delinquents. It is not necessary to assume a generic difference between persons by reason of which some are generally receptive to criminality and others not receptive. Such an assumption would be far-fetched and unjustified. There may be receptivity at a particular moment to a particular stimulation, but the elements are so complex that no generalization regarding such receptivity is possible. The closest approach to a generalization is to say that this specific receptivity is determined principally by the frequency and consistency of previous contacts with patterns of delinquency and that beyond this the delinquent behavior is adventitious.

Sixth, *cultural conflict is the underlying cause of differential association and therefore of systematic criminal behavior*. Differential association is possible because society is composed of various groups with varied cultures. These differences in culture are found in respect to many values and are generally regarded as desirable. They exist, also, with reference to the values which the laws are designed to protect, and in that form are generally regarded as undesirable. This criminal culture is as real as lawful culture and is much more prevalent than is usually believed. It is not confined to the hoodlums in slums or to professional criminals. Prisoners frequently state and undoubtedly believe that they are no worse than the majority of people on the outside. The more intricate manipulations of business and professional men may be kept within the letter of the law as interpreted but be identical in logic and effects with the criminal behavior which results in imprisonment. These practices, even if they do not result in public condemnation as crimes, are a part of the criminal culture. The more the cultural patterns conflict, the more unpredictable is the behavior of a particular person. It was possible to predict with almost complete certainty how a person reared in a Chinese village fifty years ago would behave because there was only one way for him to behave. The attempts to explain the behavior of a particular person in a modern city have been rather unproductive because the influences are in conflict and any particular influence may be very evanescent.

Seventh, *social disorganization is the basic cause of systematic criminal behavior*. The origin and the persistence of culture conflicts relating to the values expressed in the law and of differential association which is based on the cultural conflicts are due to social disorganization. Cultural conflict is a specific aspect of social disorganization and in that sense the two concepts are names for smaller and larger aspects of the same thing. But social disorganization is important in another sense. Since the law-abiding culture is dominant and more extensive, it could overcome systematic crime if organized for that purpose. But society is organized around individual and small group interests on most points. A law-abiding person is more interested in his own immediate personal projects than in abstract social welfare or justice. In this sense society permits crime to persist in systematic form. Consequently systematic crime persists not only because of differential association but also because of the reaction of the general society toward such crime. When a society or a smaller group develops a unified interest in crimes which touch its fundamental and common values, it generally succeeds in eliminating or at least greatly reducing crime. This occurred, for instance, when baseball players in the world series took bribes for throwing away a game they could have won. This affected so many people in a manner which they regarded as vital, and they reacted in such evident opposition, that the crime, so far as is known, has never been repeated. Also, when many wealthy people were kidnaped and held for ransom at the end of the prohibition period, our society reorganized the legal and administrative system in violation of the slogans and myth of state sovereignty and such kidnapings practically ceased. However, in previous times when poor and helpless people were the victims of kidnapings, as in the slave trade, impressment of sailors, shanghaiing of sailors by crimps, and unjustifiable arrests, it took generations and in some cases centuries for society to become sufficiently aware and interested to stop kidnapings in those forms. When a gang starts in a disorganized district of a city it keeps growing and other gangs develop. But when a delinquent gang started on a business street adjacent to Hyde Park, a good residential district in Chicago, the residents became concerned, formed an organization, and decided that the best way to protect themselves was by providing a club house and recreational facilities for the delinquents. This practically eliminated the gangs. Therefore, whether systematic delinquency does or does not develop is determined not only by associations that people make with the criminals, but also by the reactions of the rest of society toward systematic criminal behavior. If the society is organized with reference to the values expressed in the law, the crime is eliminated; if it is not organized, crime persists and develops. The opposition of the society may take the form of punishment, of reformation, or of prevention.

The general theory which has been presented may be summarized in the following statements: Systematic criminal behavior is due immediately to differential association in a situation in which cultural conflicts exist, and ultimately to the social disorganization in that situation. A specific or incidental crime of a particular person is due generally to the same process, but it is not possible to include all cases because of the adventitious character of delinquency when regarded as specific or incidental acts.

Bibliography

Beccaria, Cesare. *An Essay on Crimes and Punishments.* Philadelphia: Philip H. Nicklin, 1819.
Bonger, Willem Adriaan. *Criminality and Economic Conditions.* Boston: Little, Brown and Company, 1916.
Ferri, Enrico. *Criminal Sociology.* Boston: Little, Brown and Company, 1917.
Healy, William. *The Individual Delinquent.* Boston: Little, Brown and Company, 1915.
Lombroso, Cesare. *L'Uomo Delinquente.* Milan: Hoepli, 1876.
Mayhew, Henry. *London Labor and the London Poor.* London: Griffin, Bohn, and Company, 1861.
Quetelet, Adolphe. *A Treatise on Man.* Edinburgh: William and Robert Chambers, 1842.
Sellin, Thorsten. *Culture Conflict and Crime.* New York: Social Science Research Council, 1938.
Sutherland, Edwin. *Principles of Criminology.* Philadelphia: J. B. Lippincott Company, 1939.
Tarde, Gabriel. *Penal Philosophy.* Boston: Little, Brown and Company, 1912.

Among a number of works providing general historical material in criminology, the student may find the following especially useful:

de Quiros, C. Bernaldo. *Modern Theories of Criminality.* Boston: Little, Brown and Company, 1911.
Mannheim, Hermann. *Comparative Criminology.* Boston: Houghton Mifflin Company, 1965.

Mannheim, Hermann. *Pioneers in Criminology*. Chicago: Quadrangle Books, Inc., 1960.

Radzinowicz, Leon. *Ideology and Crime*. New York: Columbia University Press, 1966.

Radzinowicz, Leon. *In Search of Criminology*. Cambridge: Harvard University Press, 1962.

Vold, George. *Theoretical Criminology*. New York: Oxford University Press, 1958.

THE HERITAGE OF
MODERN CRIMINOLOGY